HUNTING COCKROACHES

A COMEDY

by Janusz Głowacki

translated by Jadwiga Kosicku

Samuel French, Inc.

JANUSZ GŁOWACKI is the author of six plays, 10 books, 20 radio plays, and four produced screenplays. His play **Cinders* was performed at the New York Shakespeare Festival's Public Theater in 1984. His novel *Give Us This Day*—about the birth of Solidarity—was banned by the Polish censor, became an underground best-seller and was published in the United States by St. Martin's Press in 1985. An earlier version of *Hunting Cockroaches* was originally produced at River Arts Repertory Theatre in Woodstock, New York.

---

*Also handled by Samuel French, Inc. Consult our *Basic Catalogue of Plays* for details.

HUNTING COCKROACHES

A COMEDY

by Janusz Głowacki

translated by Jadwiga Kosicka

SAMUEL FRENCH, INC.
45 WEST 25TH STREET   NEW YORK 10010
7623 SUNSET BOULEVARD   HOLLYWOOD 90046
LONDON   TORONTO

Copyright © 1987 by Janusz Glowacki

ALL RIGHTS RESERVED

CAUTION: Professionals and amateurs are hereby warned that HUNTING COCKROACHES is subject to a royalty. It is fully protected under the copyright laws of the United States of America, the British Commonwealth, including Canada, and all other countries of the Copyright Union. All rights, including professional, amateur, motion pictures, recitation, lecturing, public reading, radio broadcasting, television, and the rights of translation into foreign languages are strictly reserved. In its present form the play is dedicated to the reading public only.

The amateur live stage performance rights to HUNTING COCKROACHES are controlled exclusively by Samuel French, Inc., and royalty arrangements and licenses must be secured well in advance of presentation. PLEASE NOTE that amateur royalty fees are set upon application in accordance with your producing circumstances. When applying for a royalty quotation and license please give us the number of performances intended, dates of production, your seating capacity and admission fee. Royalties are payable one week before the opening performance of the play to Samuel French, Inc., at 45 W. 25th Street, New York, NY 10010; or at 7623 Sunset Blvd., Hollywood, CA 90046, or to Samuel French (Canada), Ltd., 80 Richmond Street East, Toronto, Ontario, Canada M5C 1P1.

Royalty of the required amount must be paid whether the play is presented for charity or gain and whether or not admission is charged.

Stock royalty quoted on application to Samuel French, Inc.

For all other rights than those stipulated above, apply to Bridget Aschenberg, International Creative Management, Inc., 40 W. 57th Street, New York, NY 10019.

Particular emphasis is laid on the question of amateur or professional readings, permission and terms for which must be secured in writing from Samuel French, Inc.

Copying from this book in whole or in part is strictly forbidden by law, and the right of performance is not transferable.

Whenever the play is produced the following notice must appear on all programs, printing and advertising for the play: "Produced by special arrangement with Samuel French, Inc."

Due authorship credit must be given on all programs, printing and advertising for the play.

ISBN 0 573 67048 X   Printed in U.S.A

No one shall commit or authorize any act or omission by which the copyright of, or the right to copyright, this play may be impaired.

No one shall make any changes in this play for the purpose of production.

Publication of this play does not imply availability for performance. Both amateurs and professionals considering a production are *strongly* advised in their own interests to apply to Samuel French, Inc., for written permission before starting rehearsals, advertising, or booking a theatre.

No part of this book may be reproduced, stored in a retrieval system, or transmitted in any form, by any means, now known or yet to be invented, including mechanical, electronic, photocopying, recording, videotaping, or otherwise, without the prior written permission of the publisher.

BILLING AND CREDIT REQUIREMENTS

All producers of HUNTING COCKROACHES *must* give credit to the Author in all programs and in all instances in which the title of the Play appears for purposes of advertising, publicizing or otherwise exploiting the Play and/or production. The author's name *must* appear on a separate line in which no other name appears, immediately following the title of the play, and *must* appear in size of type not less than 50% the size of title type. The name of the translator *must* be 50% of the style of type used for the name of the author.

Samuel French, Inc. can supply an *Acting with a Polish Accent Dialogue Tape and Manual* for $16.50, plus $1.24 for first-class postage and handling.

Hunting Cockroaches

By Janusz Glowacki
Translated by Jadwiga Kosicka
Directed by Lawrence Sacharow
Set by Marek Dobrowolski
Lighting by Frances Aronson
Costumes by Marianne Powell-Parker

The action takes place in one night in a Lower East Side apartment in Manhattan. There will be one intermission.

Cast

Anka Krupinski .... Elzbieta Czyzewska*
Jan Krupinski .... Olek Krupa*
Mr. Thompson, Rysio, Immigration Officer .... Ray Xifo*
Mrs. Thompson .... Deirdre O'Connell*
Czesio, Bum .... Mark Margolis*
Voice of Television Announcer .... Sean O'Brien

*Members of Actors' Equity Association. River Arts Repertory operates under the terms of a Developing Theatres Contract with Actors' Equity Association.

The taking of photographs or the making of recordings of any kind is strictly prohibited.

The audience is requested to please keep the aisle clear.

The presentation of **Hunting Cockroaches** is made possible in part by a special commissioning grant from the New York State Council on the Arts.

**MANHATTAN THEATRE CLUB
AT CITY CENTER THEATER**

Manhattan Theatre Club

Artistic Director
LYNNE MEADOW

Managing Director
BARRY GROVE

presents

HUNTING COCKROACHES

by

JANUSZ GLOWACKI

Translated by
JADWIGA KOSICKA

with

REATHEL BEAN	DAVID BERMAN	LARRY BLOCK
JOAN COPELAND	PAUL GRECO	MARTIN SHAKAR
RON SILVER	PAUL SPARER	DIANNE WIEST

Directed by
ARTHUR PENN

Sets by
HEIDI LANDESMAN

Costumes by
RITA RYACK

Lighting by
RICHARD NELSON

Sound by
STAN METELITS

Production Stage Manager
SUSIE CORDON

FEBRUARY 12 — MARCH 22, 1987

Hunting Cockroaches was originally produced by River Arts Repertory.

CAST
(in order of appearance)

She	DIANNE WIEST
He	RON SILVER
Immigration Officer	REATHEL BEAN
Rysio	DAVID BERMAN
Czesio	MARTIN SHAKAR
Bum	PAUL GRECO
Mr. Thompson	PAUL SPARER
Mrs. Thompson	JOAN COPELAND
Censor	LARRY BLOCK

PLACE
The entire action of the play takes place in a Lower East Side Manhattan apartment.

THERE WILL BE ONE INTERMISSION.

STANDBYS
Standbys will not appear without prior announcement.
For Rysio—Paul Greco; for He—David Berman.

The entire action of the play takes place in a Lower East Side Manhattan apartment.

CAST OF CHARACTERS

SHE
HE
IMMIGRATION OFFICER
CZESIO
RYSIO (RYSIU: NICKNAME)
BUM
MRS. THOMPSON
MR. THOMPSON
CENSOR

Actors may play more than one character.

Hunting Cockroaches

ACT ONE

A squalid, shabby room serving as living room, bedroom and kitchen. A door leading to the bathroom. A mildew spot in one corner of the ceiling. Two barred windows. Furniture placed haphazardly, piles of clothes here and there. An old wheelchair is clearly visible. Tea bags hang on a rope, drying. There are papers and dictionaries piled on a table by the window. Several small replicas of the Statue of Liberty stand on a shelf. A huge map of America hangs on the wall.

In the middle of the room there is a large bed. A single bare light bulb hangs directly above the bed. The light can be switched on and off by pulling a cord. HE is in the bed, asleep, unseen by the audience, with a blanket pulled over his head. Suddenly the bathroom door swings open and SHE comes out with her back toward the audience. SHE is wearing a nightgown, with a kitchen towel on her arm and a used tea-bag in her hand. Slowly and dramatically SHE starts to recite parts of Lady Macbeth's soliloquy. SHE seems to be addressing the absent Macbeth as though he were hidden in the bathtub behind the plastic curtain.

SHE. (*recites from* Macbeth *and looks at her hands*) Yet here's a spot . . . Out damned spot! Out, I say! — One; Two; Why then 'tis time to do 't! — Hell is murky! —Fie, my lord, fie! A soldier, and afeard! . . . What, will these hands ne'er be clean? — No more o' that, my lord, no more o' that: you mar all this with starting . . . Here's the smell of the blood still: all the perfumes of Arabia will not sweeten this little hand. Oh! Oh! Oh! . . . Wash your hands, put on your nightgown; look not so pale:—I tell yet again, Banquo's buried; he cannot come out of the grave . . . To bed, to bed: there's knocking at the gate. Come, come, come, come, give me your hand. What's done cannot be undone: To bed, to bed, to bed.

(*While delivering the soliloquy SHE tidies up the room; hangs the used tea-bag alongside several other ones on the rope above refrigerator then climbs up on the edge of the bathroom and hangs the kitchen towel on the curtain-rod. By the end of the soliloquy for the first time SHE turns around and seems to be taken aback by discovering the audience. A fleeting smile, half-embarrassed, half-coquettish, flashes across her face, and in an instant SHE hops into the bed, and again gives the audience a look that asks for their support.*)

HE. (*still invisible from under the covers*) Turn off the light.

SHE. (*with an impatient gesture of her hand, orders HIM to keep quiet, gets up out of bed and addresses the audience.*) My name is Anka. I can't sleep. I'm a nervous wreck. I'm Polish. I've been in New York for 3 years. For the past three months I can't get any sleep. I mean, at first I couldn't sleep for something like a month, then I could, and then I couldn't and then I could again. Now for the past forty-two days—or maybe it's twenty-two days—I can't sleep at all. (*studying the audience*) I'm an actress . . . I can't get any parts due to my accent. They say I have an awful accent . . . do I? That's my husband, Janek . . . (*points to him*) He can't sleep either. He's just pretending he's asleep. . . . (*smiles*) I know it. He can't fall asleep without his pills and I hid them. (*looks around, pulls a bottle of pills from under the mattress, and shows them to audience*) See! (*smiles triumphantly*) To tell the truth the pills don't help him any, he loves searching for them. He's a writer . . . He was very famous in Poland. . . . a novel of his came out in Paris . . . One of his plays was produced in New York. (*looks around the audience*) His name is Krupinski, Jan Krupinski. (*pauses for a moment. . . . . spelling*) K R U-P I N S K I. . . . Never heard of him? It's a good thing he's asleep. I mean, he's pretending . . . Look, I've got a whole bunch of reviews. He got a very good one in the New York Times, and a real bad one in the Village Voice. I got an award for my interpretation of Lady Macbeth in Warsaw. I know it's completely moronic but here in America you have to praise yourself, right? If you don't have any confidence in yourself, who's going to? Do I really have an awful accent? I did some work for an art critic from Poland who's well-connected. He works in an Italian restaurant at 2nd Avenue and 88th Street. He got me a temporary job at the Museum of Immigration. I'd appear every noon dressed as a nineteenth-century Polish emigrant. You know the outfit . . . babushka, boots (*ironically*). But now the museum is being repaired. . . . (*throws up her hand as if to say, "What can I do?"*) Isn't he good at pretending he's asleep. I taught him how. If it gets out he can't sleep, we're finished. In New York everybody knows how to sleep. I'm trying to get him to pretend he's happy. In New York everybody's happy. (*HE groans.*) In the day time he usually sits in front of the map. (*SHE points to the map hanging on the wall. SHE gets up, and goes over to the map, sits down in front of it, looks at the map for a while in silence.*) He can sit like this for an hour or two. (*Again SHE looks at the map in silence.*) Then he says: "What a strange country!" That's all. "What a strange country!" I told him he'd never make it here because he doesn't have a sincere smile. Everybody here has a sincere smile. And he's got a nasty one. He took it very hard. In eastern Europe nobody has a sincere smile, except drunks and informers. (*smiles*) Yesterday he sat in front of the map and practiced the art of the sincere smile, checking it every so often in the mirror. I told him he should write a play about Polish emigres, but he said the subject is boring, either you make it or you don't.

HE. (*waking or pretending to wake up*) What time it is?

SHE. (*Rapidly walks to the window, looks out into the street at the large clock on the corner.*) One hour later than usual. Lately you are asking me what time it is at 3 in the morning—now it's 4 in the morning.

HE. You are screaming again . . . Lately you scream in your sleep all the time.

SHE. Do I?

HE. You sit up in the bed and scream. (*imitates her scream*)

SHE. You'll wake up everybody in the building.

HE. Then you go back to sleep immediately.

SHE. Immediately.

HE. Immediately. But then I can't fall asleep.

SHE. Yes, I know, in the morning you have your lecture at Staten Island Community College. Where they pay you nothing, but help us with our application for the green card. And you hate your classes, because: "How can you teach Franz Kafka to students who drive to school in sport cars?" . . . All right, let's go to sleep. (*HE turns light out. They pull the blanket over their heads. Moment of silence.*) Oh my God! (*SHE turns light on.*)

HUNTING COCKROACHES

HE. What are you dreaming about?

SHE. I'm not dreaming about anything.

HE. You weren't dreaming about anything?

SHE. No. I wasn't even asleep.

HE. But why do you start screaming?

SHE. Because I felt like it.

HE. Maybe you were dreaming that we were back in Poland.

SHE. No.

HE. Or that somebody broke into the apartment through the window.

SHE. We have heavy iron bars on all the windows. No one can get through those bars.

HE. No harm checking. (*at the window, shakes the bars*) No, with those bars there, it would be impossible for anyone to get through that window. Your dreams are absolutely moronic.

SHE. (*a look of disgust on her face, whacks the floor hard with her shoe, then whacks it again*) It ran under the floorboard.

HE. Cut it out. That old bag under us will call the super. He's been waiting for a chance to get rid of us. Do you know how much he'd get for an apartment like this? Nowadays, in neighborhood like this? On the Lower East Side?

SHE. Oh, it's a terrific neighborhood all right. Some apartment. Constantly broken into, fifth floor without an elevator, cold in winter, hot in summer, and you can't put an air-conditioner in because the fuses will be blown . . .

HE. We can't afford an air-conditioner.

SHE. Muggers, rapers . . .

HE. It's a neighborhood for artists.

SHE. For cockroaches.

HE. What do you have against cockroaches? New

York is full of cockroaches. They're everywhere. Even in millionaires' houses.

SHE. How do you know? Have you ever been in a millionaire's house?

HE. Cockroaches don't spread infection and they eat only garbage. Remember Gregor?

SHE. Gregor who?

HE. The hero of Kafka's *Metamorphosis*. The one who was transformed into a cockroach. His sister used to bring him fresh rolls, cheese and milk . . . he wouldn't even spit on it. The only thing he'd touch was garbage.

SHE. I've seen them touch our caviar.

HE. Even if they did, how much food could a cockroach eat?

SHE. Then it's the rats who eat up our food.

HE. The mice.

SHE. The rats.

HE. They're big mice. Anyhow, the mice eat the cockroaches.

SHE. How do you know?

HE. I watched them.

SHE. I heard that rats eat children.

HE. We don't have any children.

SHE. Aha. . . .

HE. For God's sake, don't start that about having a baby. That's all we'd need. A baby. I want to know where we'd put it?

SHE. Over there. (*points*)

HE. And what about us?

SHE. Over here.

HE. And what about me? Where'd I do my writing?

SHE. You're not doing any writing.

HE. I have nothing to write about.

SHE. Have you ever thought about writing nursery rhymes?

HUNTING COCKROACHES

HE. Enough about baby.

SHE. That would change everything. You'd start writing. You wouldn't have any other way out.

HE. I'd always have one way out. Through the window.

SHE. With those iron bars?

HE. Let's go to sleep.

SHE. Let's. (*Humming a lullaby, "Aa, kotki dwa, szare, bure obydwa . . . " (Aa, pussycats two, both of them are black, both of them are blue . . .) with the heavy movements of a woman in the last stages of pregnancy, SHE climbs into bed and turns light out. The phone rings and wakes them up. With a start they both jump out of bed. In the process the pillow slips out from under her nightgown.*)

HE. What time it is?

SHE. Ten past four.

HE. Who could be calling at this time of night? (*HE turns light on.*)

SHE. I have no idea.

HE. Burglars? Maybe they're checking to see if we're in? (*The phone keeps ringing.*)

SHE. Well, answer it if you're so curious.

HE. Maybe it's the super. I told you not to pound on the floor. Maybe it's. . . . (*starts to whistle*)

SHE. Stop that whistling. (*HE keeps on whistling.*) You always whistle when you're afraid of something. I can't stand it any longer. Maybe it's who?

HE. KGB?

SHE. KGB?

HE. To scare me.

SHE. But why would they want to scare you?

HE. Because they know I hate them. Because I'm a writer, an emigre writer and I could write something.

SHE. But you're not writing anything.

HE. But I could start writing at any time.

SHE. Then start.

HE. But I don't have anything to write about.

SHE. Why would they want to scare you? You're already scared of them. Maybe it's the Immigration Office.

HE. What for?

SHE. I don't know. Maybe someone squealed on us.

HE. Squealed about what?

SHE. That our visas expired.

HE. But they promised we'd get green cards.

SHE. But we didn't get them yet. We've still got to go for another interrogation.

HE. It's not an interrogation, it's an interview. The fact that we got the notice to go means that everything's fine. Millions of people in New York are just waiting for that.

SHE. To go for an interrogation?

HE. To go for an interview. (*The phone keeps ringing.*)

SHE. Maybe someone's calling from Europe? The time's different there. What time it is in Europe now?

HE. What time it is here?

SHE. Quarter past four.

HE. Then in Europe it must be . . .

SHE. In the morning?

HE. Yes.

SHE. Then it has to be someone from Europe.

HE. Andrzej is in France. Maybe he's calling. But just what do you think he wants from us? Oh, I know, of course. He is jealous.

SHE. Jealous? Of what?

HE. What do you mean of what? He emigrated only to Paris, and I am in New York, and I made it here.

SHE. But you didn't make it.

HE. But he doesn't know it. Maybe we should answer the phone.

SHE. Maybe we should. (*Bending over the telephone, they wordlessly encourage each other to pick up the receiver. Just at the moment HE reaches for it, the phone stops ringing.*)

HE. Damn it, why did you tell me not to answer it? Now it's too late. (*The phone starts to ring again, twice only.*)

(*A typical immigration OFFICER crawls from under the bed. He spreads his papers and leafs through them. He's a very nice little bureaucrat and smiles radiantly throughout the interview.*)

OFFICER. Would you come over here. Both of you, please. (*The immigration OFFICER takes their fingerprints, looks at Jan's legs.*) What wrong with your leg? Aren't you limping a bit?

HE. No, I'm not. My leg just fell asleep.

OFFICER. Aha . . . Now your turn, lady. Thank you. That's all.

HE. Immigration asks everyone the same questions.

SHE. Absolutely everyone?

OFFICER. (*To HER*) Do you intend to engage in prostitution while you're in the United States?

HE. Take it as a compliment.

OFFICER. You haven't answered my question yet.

SHE. No, of course not, I don't intend to. But if I may . . .

OFFICER. Thank you. (*to him*) Did you come to America with the intention of killing the President of the United States? (*HE clears his throat.*)

SHE. Is that a standard question?

OFFICER. I'm waiting for your answer.

HE. No. To tell the truth . . . I don't understand.

OFFICER. Thank you. (*puts his papers away*) No more questions. That's all we wanted to know. (*takes a step toward the bed, then stops*) One more question. Have you ever been treated for VD?

SHE. What kind of VD?

OFFICER. That's exactly what I'm asking you.

SHE. No, never.

OFFICER. (*To him*) And you?

HE. No, never.

OFFICER. Thank you. You'll be notified when to appear for the next interview.

HE. Spytaj o pieniądze.

SHE. Excuse me, sir.

OFFICER. Yes?

SHE. Is it possible to obtain a temporary work permit? You see, we're in some financial difficulties, nothing serious but . . .

OFFICER. Sorry, that's impossible. But I don't want you to worry. As long as you don't work without a permit, you can sleep in peace.

HE. Thank you very much.

SHE. Thank you very much.

OFFICER. Not at all. Good luck to you. (*OFFICER starts folding papers, disappears under bed.*)

HE AND SHE. Good luck to you.

SHE. What I'd really like to know is whether they think that if you'd come to kill the President you'd give them an honest answer. (*SHE turns light out.*) Is crabs a venereal disease?

HE. You never mentioned to me that you had crabs.

SHE. Oh, I am mentioning it now to keep the conversation going. (*HE turns light on.*)

HE. Interesting. I have no idea whether crabs is a venereal disease or not. I never gave it much thought. (*Phone rings three times.*) In Poland once I met a guy who'd spent five years in prison, and I wanted you to know he told me he was really glad to have a rat in his cell. They became friends.

SHE. You told me the same story before, but last time the guy was really glad to have a spider in his cell.

HE. I'm sure I said it was a rat, the spider was in a Dumas book. *The Count of Monte Cristo, Part II.* (*Roach crawls across bed, HE whacks it away and stomps on floor to scare it.*) That cockroach was the size of a sparrow.

SHE. Get it.

HE. It got away—into the cracks in the floor. It ran into the cracks because that's where they do their hatching. They hunt at night and hatch eggs during the day. It's interesting, cockroaches don't like coffee. (*From the floor below comes the sound of pounding on the ceiling with a broom.*) Oh God, how I hate that old hag. She gets excited at the slightest sound. Why doesn't she go to sleep? When I saw that old hag for the first time, and she threatened to call the police, I understood for the first time in Dostoyevsky's *Crime and Punishment* it's not just a theoretical problem about whether killing one's fellow man is ever justified and under what circumstances. I bet Dostoyevsky lived in a building in St. Petersburg with an old hag like that directly underneath him, and that's how he got the idea. Cockroaches are fast learners. There's no doubt about it. It's strange that there aren't any cockroaches in Poland. Maybe they locked them up somewhere? Or maybe they sent all the cockroaches off to take an indoctrination course? The older ones are much more cunning. The younger ones don't run for cover if you turn the light on. See! (*demonstrates*) I'm talking about the littlest ones.

SHE. The babies.

HE. All the older, smarter ones run straight under the boards. I wonder why cockroaches don't like coffee. (*mounting sound of a siren*)

SHE. That's the same one as yesterday. Recognize it? Now here's where it gets stuck. There, it's just the same as yesterday.

HE. All the sirens sound the same.

SHE. That's the one we heard yesterday. Do you hear that? Now it goes way down in the lower register.

HE. You're talking nonsense. Let's go to sleep.

SHE. I'm telling you. That siren has a personality all its own. It's trying something fancy. Usually it goes "uuuuu" not with this "buuuum." Maybe he's trying to give us a clue about something.

HE. That there's a fire somewhere. Listen, will you, I have to get up early for my lecture.

SHE. I know. You have to lecture about Franz Kafka to girls who drive to school in Mitsubishis. Kafka would have a good laugh. You simply envy them their Mitsubishis.

HE. I won't fall asleep. (*HE switches off light.*) I know I won't be able to fall asleep. (*A moment of silence. Then suddenly SHE says . . .*)

SHE. Milk!

HE. Oh no! (*SHE turns on light.*)

SHE. Milk is good for sleeping. Cold milk.

HE. What are you talking about?

SHE. I meant to say hot milk. Hot milk helps you get to sleep.

HE. I hate milk. Especially hot milk. I love cold milk. You look awful. Actually you look green.

SHE. I can't sleep.

HE. Neither can I.

SHE. I know. You look like a corpse.

HE. Like a corpse?

SHE. That's right. I'm sure hot milk would do us both a lot of good.

HE. Didn't we already try hot milk?

SHE. Yes. (*HE turns light out. They put the blanket over their heads. They lie in silence for a couple of moments.*)

SHE. I didn't ghink you;d ever have the nerve to go up there.

HE. I got on the elevator. I got off at the 19th floor. They're on several floors.

SHE. I didn't know that.

HE. The 19th, the 21st and the 23rd.

SHE. Three whole floors? (*SHE turns light on.*)

HE. Three whole floors!

SHE. I hope you got there just before noon.

HE. Why?

SHE. That's the best time to go see Americans. Just before lunchtime when they're about to get something to eat.

HE. Here in America nobody asks what you had for lunch, but who you had lunch with. That's why I got there at two.

SHE. Aha.

HE. There's a dirty old corridor. On the right, behind a glass window there's a receptionist acting as a guard. Just like at police headquarters. (*laughs*) A blonde. Not half-bad.

SHE. Was she young?

HE. Very.

SHE. Wearing glasses?

HE. Why do you ask?

SHE. I just thought she might be wearing glasses.

HE. No, she wasn't wearing glasses. I thought the office

of such an influential magazine would look quite different.

SHE. Like what?

HE. I thought there'd be antiques, old china, flowers, Chagall's paintings, everything in good taste. But their walls look just like our walls. I went over to her.

SHE. Over to whom?

HE. To the guard. The blonde. I smiled.

SHE. (*frowning*) You didn't have to do that.

HE. (*irritated*) That's where you're wrong. She liked my smile. She smiled back. Not everyone thinks the way you do. (*HE flashes a prolonged and sincere smile. Then the smile fades away.*)

SHE. Well, well. . . .

HE. So I said that I'd like to see the editor.

SHE. Aha.

HE. Then she looked me over carefully.

SHE. She looked you over carefully?

HE. Very careful. And she said she was sorry but that it was impossible . . .

SHE. Impossible.

HE. Then I told her everything about myself. And she smiled again.

SHE. Did she call the editor?

HE. No. She went out for a little bit. Then she came back and said the editor would see me immediately.

SHE. Immediately?

HE. That's right, see me immediately. You can imagine how I felt.

SHE. Yes. And what happened?

HE. The editor saw me.

SHE. The editor himself?

HE. The editor himself.

SHE. What was his name?

HUNTING COCKROACHES 21

HE. I don't remember.

SHE. Didn't he give you his card?

HE. He doesn't have to have a card. Does Reagan need a card?

SHE. No, he doesn't need a card.

HE. Or does the Pope?

SHE. Personally, I deeply admire the Pope. Unfortunately he is a little bit too religious.

HE. I introduced myself. He asked me to sit down and he told me he's very interested in me, Poland, Solidarity and Lech Walesa.

SHE. Did he give you a cup of coffee?

HE. Yes, and I gave him my story.

SHE. Did he take it?

HE. Of course. He said he was glad to have it, and that I should call him in two weeks.

SHE. In two weeks?

HE. That's a very short time. You have no idea how long it usually takes. Then I apologized. For taking up his time like that.

SHE. What did he say?

HE. He just laughed . . . But it was a quick laugh. (*demonstrates how*)

SHE. That's quick. But don't worry. All Americans in responsible positions laugh quickly so as not to waste time. He must have liked you.

HE. (*smiles happily*) You know, I think he did.

SHE. That's great. Once we get money we'll move uptown. To 4th Street. It's much safer there. The floors are thicker, you can smash cockroaches and they don't hear you downstairs.

HE. Don't get excited. (*He turns light out.*)

SHE. I know perfectly well that you didn't go anywhere, that you chickened out and that you feel bad about it, that you think you're dumb, and that you hate yourself. You didn't see the editor, and I even suspect you didn't get as far as the elevator.

HE. (*turns light on*) Look at me. Do you see what I look like? (*sits on bed*) Do you see?

SHE. (*looks him over carefully*) Yes, I see.

HE. And?

SHE. And what?

HE. I mean, how could I have gone there in the state I'm in. You can see for yourself . . . You said it: I look like a very sick man.

SHE. Oh no, like a corpse. I said you look like a corpse.

HE. It's because I don't get enough sleep.

SHE. I know.

HE. I constantly bump into things, the buttons on my shirt come off, I spill my coffee, I can't go and have a drink with anyone because I'll spill it as soon as I try to take a sip. It isn't even that what I say is such nonsense, but I say it at the wrong times before I should or when it's too late; what I want to say would be just fine if I only knew the right moment to say it. Anyone who looks at me can see that I don't get enough sleep.

SHE. So what? I bet that Kafka didn't get enough sleep either, and actually the great German philosopher Max Scheler died from insomnia.

HE. Well, that's just why nobody would ever take them seriously here.

SHE. Have a glass of milk.

HE. I took an elevator to the 17th floor, I went over to the secretary, I looked at her, she looked at me, and it all became clear.

SHE. What?

HE. We're both insomniacs.

SHE. Don't bite your nails.

HUNTING COCKROACHES

HE. That's exactly it, she bit her nails too. We looked at each other and we both bit our nails.

SHE. And then what happened?

HE. And then I noticed that she had a button missing on her blouse and she noticed that one of my pockets was torn. While she was trying to fix her blouse, she spilled her coffee. And I tried to hide my torn pocket, but then my manuscript went all over the floor. There wasn't a chance she'd let me get through.

SHE. Why not?

HE. Insomniacs have fear and contempt for other insomniacs. Only a sleeper can help me. Sound sleepers run New York, the problem is how to get to them. Insomniacs won't let you, they are very crafty. They pretend, and look well rested. They dress very carefully, they put make-up under their eyes. Only their movements give them away.

SHE. What movements?

HE. (*knocks an empty glass to the floor*) And they boast too much about what a good night's sleep they've had. No more than 10 per cent of all the people in New York sleep.

SHE. Why is that?

HE. Because of the emigres coming here. What do you think of my theory?

SHE. I think you've gone crazy.

HE. Once I had a chance to get into the world of real sleepers. The Thompsons were ready to introduce me.

SHE. Don't start that again.

HE. You ruined all my chances. You behaved like a barbarian.

SHE. I know. I know it all by heart. I wonder how long you're going to keep pestering me about that? I really . . .

HE. I want you to know that I'm unable to sleep, that I pace back and forth in the room and (*HE demonstrates.*) that I bump into the wardrobe, there, you see! I'm not fit to live, and it's all thanks to you. (*He goes over to the wheelchair standing in the corner, slumps into it, and rolls to the front of the stage.*)

SHE. What do you have to say about that?

HE. And just what does that wheelchair have to do with it?

SHE. If only you hadn't brought that wheelchair home . . . You came home very pleased with yourself that day. You'd met Tomek in a wheelchair going off to work. You asked him what was wrong with him, and he said there was nothing wrong with him, he just bought himself a wheelchair to avoid paying the rent. A landlord has no right to evict an invalid, that's right isn't it? And the next day you brought home that wheelchair.

HE. It was in very good shape. I found it thrown out on the street as trash.

SHE. You wanted me to pretend to be an invalid and spend the rest of my life in a wheelchair.

HE. What makes you think that? That's absurd.

SHE. Then why did you bring it home? Answer me that!

HE. It's a nice comfortable wheelchair. In mint condition. It could be the pride of any home.

SHE. Why did you say you were curious to find out whether I'd know how to use it? (*Furious, SHE grabs the back of the wheelchair and stops it from rolling.*)

HE. Out of curiosity. Do you really think I'd make you spend the rest of your life in a wheelchair? Just to save 350 dollars a month?

SHE. Of course, I do. You'd make me do it to save even 5 dollars a month. (*SHE pushes him into the bathroom, slamming the door.*)

HE. 350 dollars is a lot of money. (*HE reappears from the bathroom.*)

SHE. Do you want to go back to Poland?

HE. I don't know.

SHE. We can't go back.

HE. I know. (*pause*) I'll go to the magazine. (*pause*) Tomorrow.

SHE. You won't ever go, so stop lying to yourself—and to me. You've always lied to me.

HE. No I haven't. Not in Poland.

SHE. Didn't you read me T. S. Eliot's *Wasteland* and say you wrote it?

HE. I wanted only the best for you. My poems weren't as good. I loved you.

SHE. Listen, there's one thing I want you to do for me. All the Polish emigres here are going crazy. I implore you: don't lie. Or you'll start to believe your own lies. Like Krzysiek who believes he's making a movie, and Grazyna who's convinced she's working for CBS. You'll end up like that. You'll jump off the George Washington Bridge.

HE. Don't worry. To get there you need a car. (*The phone starts ringing again. SHE automatically picks up the receiver.*)

SHE. Hello, oh, it's you Zosia. Zosia is calling from Queens. Yes it's late, but this is New York, no? You're lucky you reached us. We went to the theatre and then to eat Chinese as usual. Did we call you before? No? Did you call us? No reason, I'm really glad you called. What? Wlodek sold six paintings? That's wonderful, congratulations. (*pause*) A whole article in *The Times*? That's wonderful. I mean, he certainly deserves it. If you're good enough, you'll always make it. It takes talent and hard work. We? Jan was at the *New Yorker* today, the editor had heard about him, loves his work, he was really glad to meet Janek. For sure we didn't call you before. Are you sure you didn't call us? Have a nice day. It was great talking to you. Love to Wlodek from both of us. (*SHE finishes the conversation and puts the receiver down. They both sit in silence for a while.*)

HE. It's a strange country. (*The mounting sound of a fire siren. SHE grows animated.*)

SHE. There it goes again. A real artist. (*SHE turns out the light.*) What are we going to do?

HE. I don't know. (*HE begins looking for something.*)

SHE. What are you looking for?

HE. Sleeping pills.

SHE. I'll help you. (*They look together for a while.*)

HE. There were at least ten pills left in the bottle.

SHE. What happened to it?

HE. It was here by the bed.

SHE. Maybe in the bathroom?

HE. They were standing by the bed. (*They continue looking for the pills. HE pulls out things from the drawer of a nightstand.*) Look what I find here: your amber jewelry and a leather bound edition of *Faust*. You were going to sell them when we first got here, and the caviar too.

SHE. I was going to sell *Faust* as the last resort.

HE. This is the last resort.

SHE. Nobody wants to buy this old *Faust*.

HE. That's because it's in German. And nobody wants to buy the caviar because it's Danish. In Poland, I asked you specifically to get Russian caviar. (*HE's looking for the pills.*) The restaurant is called the Russian Tea Room, not the Danish Tea Room.

SHE. Don't look there, you won't find them there. (*The sound of a fire siren again. It is a slightly different sound. HE finds pills.*)

SHE. That's not ours. Yesterday a pigeon tried to peck my eyes out.

HE. Oh, my God, go to sleep.

SHE. I went out to buy some milk and left the window open . . .

HE. I told you, always close the windows before you go out.

SHE. I came back and there was this pigeon sitting on this table pecking at a potato . . . I went over to it, the pigeon looked directly at me, spread it's wings, opened its beak and hissed.

HE. Hissed? You mean, cooed?

SHE. No cooed, hissed. Then he raised up one of its legs with claws on it . . .

HE. Claws?

SHE. Claws. It tried to peck my eyes out.

HE. (*in despair, without the will to resist*) Oh, my God.

SHE. I got scared. And then the pigeon stopped pecking at the potato and slowly hopped over to the window. But you know, I understand that pigeon. It has to be like that. It wouldn't survive otherwise. And I wanted to tell you that everybody's got to behave like that pigeon. Scientists have proved that New York babies are born with thicker eardrums, smaller lungs and more hair in their noses than the average Colorado baby. So as to muffle the sound and inhale less air. You see, they naturally acquire an antipollution defense system. They grow more hair in their noses, the windpipe through which the air goes to their lungs get shorter, their skin becomes thicker and their nails harder. That's what the latest research has shown. (*HE turns light out.*)

HE. Let's go to sleep.

SHE. My tooth hurts. This one here. (*SHE points to it.*)

HE. That means someone in your family will get sick.

SHE. It hurts a lot.
HE. Take an aspirin. There are four left. (*SHE turns light on.*)
SHE. I have to go to the dentist.
HE. Take two now and two more in an hour.
SHE. It's a front tooth.
HE. Don't get upset. Teeth often hurt when you're under nervous stress.
SHE. You said that Zbyszek promised to lend us 200 dollars . . . Go ask him.
HE. OK, I'll go.
SHE. Go today.
HE. Okay, I'll go.
SHE. Hey, you should write a play about Zbyszek. He worked in a shipyard in Gdansk, then he got arrested, was beaten up, sent to prison. He managed to escape, when they caught him they said, prison, or leave the country. He came to America and now he's got a job renovating the Statue of Liberty . . .
HE. It sounds like socialist realism.
SHE. Americans will love it.
HE. Who'll be interested in that? Maybe if he were Russian.
SHE. OK, so make him a Russian . . . Just imagine a vicious snow storm, full moon, the waves are rolling, and he's standing right in the torch at the top of the Statue of Liberty, singing . . . in Russian. Now that's something for Broadway. I've got to go to the dentist.
HE. Look how lucky Zbyszek was. They knocked his teeth out in prison. Now he doesn't have any more problems with the dentist.
SHE. I'm worried about our apartment in Warsaw.
HE. Why? They took it away from us.

(*They lie for several moments trying to sleep. Two plain-*

clothes policemen crawl out from under the bed. The first one (RYSIO) stocky and grim. The second (CZESIO) talkative.)

RYSIO. It's clean under the bed, nothing suspicious there. (*dusts himself off*)

SHE. Have you got a search warrant?

CZESIO. But who's conducting a search here? Don't take it to heart, Rysiu. Rise above it, let them be insulting if they want to. How do you like the apartment, Rysiu?

RYSIO. (*contemptuously*) It stinks.

CZESIO. Don't turn up your nose, Rysiu. It's in the best part of Warsaw. Three rooms with a kitchen, and the windows have a southern exposure, don't they?

SHE. That's right, but just what are you getting at?

RYSIO. The terrace is too small.

CZESIO. Don't be so fussy, Rysiu. Look at how big the bedroom is. (*HE whistles.*)

RYSIO. After work, a guy wants to sit on the terrace with a bottle, have a drink and think life over.

SHE. Stop it, will you.

CZESIO. The layout is not half bad. Look, you can take those bookshelves out, and you've got plenty of room.

RYSIO. It stinks. That villa that belonged to the doctor suited me better. It had a garden.

CZESIO. The captain has his eye on the villa. I'm telling you, you'd better take it. For a writer, you're pretty good at whistling, pal. That's what makes artists artists.

SHE. Look here, we were searched two weeks ago. (*RYSIO starts to emit strange sounds.*) What's wrong with him?

CZESIO. Nothing, that's just the way he laughs.

RYSIO. Can I rough her up a bit?

CZESIO. Take it easy, Rysiu, it's not worth getting worked up. My God, you'd think we were dealing with some real slobs, but she's a famous actress, a great artist. When we were going through that architect's apartment on Miodowa Street this morning he started acting up. So Rysiu roughed him up a bit, and you know what, my friends, it's hard to believe that a supposedly cultured man with the benefit of a college education would scream like that: we felt embarrassed for him.

SHE. What apartment are you two talking about? If you've got this apartment in mind let me point out that this apartment's taken, that should be obvious.

CZESIO. What's the point of pretending? I mean, why all this make-believe? Can't we talk this over like grown-ups? I mean, isn't it obvious you're going on a long trip?

SHE. Where to?

CZESIO. You're emigrating.

SHE. I don't know what you're talking about.

CZESIO. All the Jews are leaving.

SHE. We're not Jews.

CZESIO. We are the ones to decide that.

RYSIO. Excuse me, please can I use your phone? (*SHE laughs and shrugs her shoulders.*)

CZESIO. Just what are you scribbling there, pal? Maybe you want to lodge a written complaint against us, eh? (*amused*) Hear that, Rysiu?

RYSIO. This is your little doggy calling.

CZESIO. Give your wife a hug from me.

RYSIO. The sarge says hello. He'd like to shake your shaggy little paw. . . . The wife sends her best greetings . . . I can hardly hear you, my pet.

CZESIO. That's because the line is bugged. Dial 11 and get them to turn it off for a while.

RYSIO. I'll call you right back, my pet.

CZESIO. How can anyone live in a country like this? Ransacking people's apartments, censorship, a total lack of freedom and justice, erosion of one's moral principles.

Whereas you'll be sitting pretty in New York, living it up in Manhattan, all the Scotch you can drink . . . And the CIA finances the whole thing, lunch with Susan Sontag, then in the evening as it's getting dark the aliens come down on flying saucers. I wouldn't mind going there myself, but somebody has to stay here and maintain order . . .

RYSIO. Hello, Lieutenant Marciniak? Sergeant Rysio speaking. Listen, stop bugging the number I'm calling from for a half-hour, OK? Yeah, the terrace's too small. Thanks.

(*RYSIO calls his wife. RYSIO and CZESIO speak simultaneously.*)

RYSIO. Hello pet! Yes, now I can hear you perfectly, honey.

CZESIO. Of course, it's a terrible loss for the country. A real brain drain . . . all those scientists and artists going abroad.

RYSIO. Yeah, there are four big rooms . . .

CZESIO. It's like chopping off your own hand . . .

RYSIO. Excuse me, lady, the wife wants to know if the heating works good in winter? (*SHE nods affirmatively.*) She says it works good. But there aren't any cabinets in the kitchen.

CZESIO. There was this artist — he said he loved his country and he refused to leave, and then all of a sudden it turns out that he was a Japanese spy. He got 25 years. Ever been to Japan?

HE. No, only to Bulgaria.

RYSIO. The windows are large, some of them double. And there's a TV set. Excuse me, but the wife wants to know if it's a color TV?

SHE. It's black and white.

Rysio. How come? (*SHE shrugs her shoulders. Rysio on the phone, very disappointed*) Listen my pet, I'm sorry to say it's black and white, can you imagine that! (*CZESIO turns on TV set.*)

Voice of the Announcer. Yesterday a tiny band of twenty thousand CIA agents disguised as workers came out on the streets of Warsaw, brandishing emblems of the long defunct trade union SOLIDARITY and displaying petty bourgeois antisocialist slogans demanding bread, meat, the reduction of prices and the establishment of equality and justice. The outraged citizens of Warsaw on their own initiative called for the forces of law and order to use water cannons and tear gas to disperse the mob . . .

Rysio. The picture's good, honey . . .

Czesio. There's just a little distortion, wait, I'll try the other channel . . . (*CZESIO changes the channel.*)

Voice of Announcer. demanding bread, meat the reduction of prices and the establishment of equality and justice. The outraged citizens of Warsaw on their own initiative called for the forces of law and order to use water cannons and tear gas to disperse the mob . . .

Rysio. Yes, now it's much better. Gotta get back to work. (*CZESIO turns the TV off.*)

He. I'm not leaving anywhere. I have a right to stay here. (*the whistle of the teapot*) I'm going to make some tea.

Czesio. Could we have a cup of tea too before we leave? (*HE gives out the tea bags for CZESIO, RYSIO, then gets two cups for HE and SHE and pours the water.*)

Rysio. (*to her*) The wife wanted me to ask you for your autograph. We've seen all your movies, you're wearing the same nightgown.

He. Sign it for her.

HUNTING COCKROACHES

SHE. (*signing the autograph*) What's your wife's first name?

RYSIO. Katarzyna. (*HE prepares tea for himself and for HER. The foursome sitting on the bed in total silence dip their tea-bags in their cups, keeping the same rhythm and tempo.*)

CZESIO. Look, it's Lipton's. You know I really like you, just tell me one thing. You look smart, why do you write?

HE. Why? (*They stop dipping tea bags.*)

CZESIO. A smart man never writes, a smart man never leaves any trace behind him. (*RYSIO and CZESIO crawl under the bed, taking their tea along with them.*)

SHE. When they came, we had no idea we were going to emigrate. (*HE nods affirmatively.*) But *they* already knew. I wonder how?

CZESIO. (*disappearing under the bed*) Rysiu, did you hear that? She wonders how we knew. (*RYSIO's peculiar laugh can be heard from beneath the bed.*)

SHE. (*SHE begins to massage his back, kisses him.*) Listen, why don't you call that director?

HE. You mean John?

SHE. He really liked your last play, he wanted to do something with it.

HE. Oh, you're just saying that.

SHE. He really is a good director.

HE. Oh, come on, what's the point of it, it's a waste of time talking to him. The guy's a nervous wreck, he can't pull himself together. He hasn't been able to finish anything for the past few years. He's finished creatively. They say he hasn't been able to get a decent night's sleep for over two years! He's Czechoslovakian. (*SHE continues sensual massage, kisses him.*) Oh, no. I'm not going to fall for that. (*HE tries to get out of her clutches,*

SHE holds him tight. They struggle.)

SHE. What's the matter?

HE. Oh no. I know very well what's on your mind.

SHE. (*HE tries to get out of her grip, but SHE holds him tight, pushing against the iron head-board of the bed. While the struggle continues, they carry on their conversation.*) What would be the harm in having a baby?

HE. Where would we put it?

SHE. Over there.

HE. And what about us?

SHE. Over here.

HE. Where would I do my writing?

SHE. You're not doing any writing.

HE. I have nothing to write about.

SHE. Write about me.

HE. About you?

SHE. About me.

HE. But what about you?

SHE. Write what you think about me.

HE. There is nothing interesting about you.

SHE. O.K. So write what you really think about me.

HE. It wouldn't make any difference.

SHE. If you'd only written a sentence a day, it would have amounted to, 365 times 3 years, minus Sunday, 939 sentences, that makes at least the first act of a play. (*addressing the audience directly.*) No?

BLACKOUT

INTERMISSION

ACT TWO

SHE's lying under the sheets. HE's in a chair studying the map; nearby is a can of roach spray.

HE. What a strange country. I was born in a town that was Polish once, then it was Czech, then it was Austrian, then it was Russian, then it was German, and now it's Communist. When Stalin died, during a memorial ceremony at our school the principal informed us that the leaders of the Polish People's Republic had decided to honor the memory of the best friend Polish children ever had by renaming our school *Stalinowka* and the town to Stalinowo. So I suggested our principal also be renamed Joseph Stalin. The colonel in the Secret Police who interrogated me really liked the idea of renaming our principal to Stalin. I was lucky. He not only saved me from prison but he showed a lot of interest in my career, until he was transferred to Rome as an expert on religious affairs. (*demonstrates*) Here's France, and Austria, and Germany, the Soviet Union, Poland. The boundary lines between all the countries twist, and turn, and twitch like worms in a can. Messy. (*points to the map*) That's what you call a neat job. Look here. (*points to states on the map and then to other states, all of which are rectangular in shape, making appropriate gestures all the while*) Montana, Wyoming, North Dakota, South Dakota . . . Missouri (*HE pronounces it "misery."*) This country was laid out by someone who had technical training. (*SHE appears.*) Buildings, (*traces rectangles in the air*) streets, (*traces lines*) everything, even people are well made. That's what you'd call a good piece of work. Only the cockroaches seem not to have come out quite right . . . yet.

SHE. You're not going to use that are you? (*HE crosses away from the map.*) It's a terrible poison. You know Malgosia. The most successful Polish actress ever. She was a bartender at this little bar on the corner of 7th Street and First Avenue. They happened to be making a Miller beer commercial there. And they went into ecstasies over her. Shortly afterwards she married a producer, then she left him for another producer. Now she's got a role in a full-length movie, is modeling for *Vogue*. Do you know what she told me? She told me never to use that spray. She personally uses only that white powder sprinkled evenly along the walls. The powder poisons them slowly, dazes them. They start moving slower and slower, and slower. The powder eats through their shell. And then they start reeling like drunks and then they die. It kills the eggs too. And to think that when I played Lady Macbeth in Warsaw, she was only the third witch. (*HE turns out light.*) I was in the park yesterday.

HE. We stayed home all day long yesterday. The last time we went out was Sunday.

SHE. I was in the park Sunday.

HE. What for?

SHE. It was dark already.

HE. What park?

SHE. In our park. The Tompkins Square Park between Avenue A and B. (*HE turns light on.*)

HE. You mean to tell me you actually went in the park after dark?

SHE. That's right.

HE. I don't believe you.

SHE. The place was swarming with people.

HE. I know, and the only thing you're afraid of is empty streets. What have you got against empty streets? If there's no one on the street, no one is going to harm you. Do you remember that time on Orchard Street you were so scared because it was absolutely empty? Then you breathed a sign of relief when at last you spotted a human being. And that was the human being who mugged us. How could you go in the park after dark?

SHE. They think the park is quite safe.

HE. What they?

SHE. The people who live in the park.

HE. How am I supposed to do any writing if you keep telling me things like that?

SHE. I went to the park because you don't do any writing.

HE. Didn't anyone bother you?

SHE. No.

HE. You were lucky. (*HE turns light out.*)

SHE. But I picked up someone. (*HE turns light on.*)

HE. What for?

SHE. Out of fear.

HE. Fear of what?

SHE. That we're going to end up in the park eventually.

HE. The park is populated only by crazy people, drunks, drug addicts, and gangsters.

SHE. No, the gangsters are in Chicago.

BUM. (*The voice of the BUM coming from under the bed:*) Neurosis.

HE. What?

(*The BUM starts to crawl out from under the bed.*)

BUM. Your wife is neurotic. (*He climbs onto the bed and starts to scratch himself.*) Just take a look at her. You should be more considerate of her feelings. I don't think she's happy.

HE. Why?

BUM. Last night I saw her in the park talking to herself.

HE. Yesterday we stayed home all day long.

BUM. You're right. I saw her last Sunday. (*scratches himself more and more energetically*) Don't worry, it's the mange, not fleas.

HE. Oh, I see.

BUM. You don't look too peppy yourself. Do you booze?

HE. No, I just can't sleep.

BUM. Too bad. I thought you might have a small bottle hidden away somewhere.

HE. So you're an alcoholic.

BUM. That's right. Bedspreads are all right, but after two days of steady rain, they're finished. Disposable items are always preferable. (*points to back issues of the Times scattered all over the room*) Take these foot warmers along. (*BUM wraps paper around Jan's feet. HE eyes the foot warmers dubiously, walks about trying them out.*) It's a very wise decision on your part. Why are you afraid of living in the park, children? Our park, it's the best park in the city. The only ideal location, if you plan to stay in Manhattan, of course.

SHE. What are you talking about? What park? What do you need any park for? We've got an apartment. We're paying rent . . . (*The BUM lifts his head up and looks at her questioningly.*) Well, as a matter of fact, we are behind on our payment but only for the last month's rent . . . (*After a moment, the BUM looks up again.*) . . . OK, for the last two months . . . Besides, Zbyszek has promised to lend us the last two months.

BUM. (*pointing to the TV set*) Oh, there's my stool. (*He gets up from the bed and sits on the TV set.*)

SHE. You're smashing our TV set.

BUM. This stool of mine stood for an entire week on the corner of 5th Street and Avenue B.

HE. I told you we shouldn't have taken that TV set off the street. I knew we'd get into trouble because of it.

SHE. Don't butt into this, I'm going to deal with him . . . All right, I admit it, I took that TV set off the street. I'm not the least ashamed to have *one* item in my apartment that was picked out of the trash on the sidewalk. (*The BUM taps on the chair with his finger.*) Well, OK, maybe two items. (*The BUM points to the table.*)

SHE. And the table, so what?! Most young couples in New York furnish their apartments out of the trash found on the sidewalks. Thanks to that (*points to TV set*) we could watch the birthday party for the Statue of Liberty.

BUM. It's a good thing you chose our park. A lot of beginners are taken in by the charms of Central Park.

SHE. I already told you we're not going to any park. (*Meanwhile HE turns his back on the BUM and puts the blanket over his head.*)

BUM. To be perfectly honest with you, the view in Central Park is better, but the police there wake you up all the time and push your feet off the bench, and make you smile for the tourists taking pictures. You're under a lot of stress there.

SHE. (*to Jan*) What are you up to?

HE. I'm ignoring him.

SHE. Well, do something.

HE. Let's go to bed and pretend he's not here. Come close and pull the covers up! (*SHE gets into bed next to him. They pull the covers up.*)

BUM. The people who go to live in Central Park run out of steam after a month or two. And move to Washington Square, but sooner or later, when they can't keep it up any longer, they end up in our park.

HE. (*from under the covers*) That's what comes of your clever ideas about picking people up.

SHE. (*from under the covers*) I can't take it any longer.

HE. (*from under the covers*) Let's show him we've got class.

SHE. (*from under the covers*) Look, I'm shaking all over.

HE. (*from under the covers*) Don't let yourself to be taken in. Just keep calm. (*Suddenly HE jumps up in a rage, tossing the covers aside.*) What's going on here? I have a lecture in the morning. Stop talking all that rubbish. You don't have any right to be here.

SHE. Calm down.

HE. (*runs over to the wardrobe*) Look over here. (*HE struggles with it, without being able to open the door.*)

BUM. A cabinet like that should be attacked from the bottom. Then it'll open. (*Jan follows the BUM's instructions in attacking the door. The wardrobe opens. HE looks for something inside.*) That cabinet used to be located between 2nd and 3rd Street at Avenue C. I used it in October when it rained so much. (*Meanwhile Jan finds his jacket and takes his wallet out of the pocket. HE goes over to the BUM.*)

HE. Look at this. It's my PEN membership card. This is for the Dramatists Guild, and this is for the Authors League of America.

BUM. Sssshhhh. Did you hear that?

HE. What was it?

BUM. A Mercedes just went by. That's the second one this week. I've sighted a BMW recently.

HE. (*lowering his voice*) Are you afraid of the Germans too?

BUM. The neighborhood is getting gentrified. The rents will go up. (*His eyes darting about, the BUM comes forward to the front of the stage, crouches behind a chair, pulls a pint bottle of liquor out of his hip pocket, and takes a gulp.*)

SHE. Oh, my God . . . Zyrardow . . .

HE. Are you starting that all over again?

SHE. (*SHE goes over to the BUM, falls to her knees on the other side of the chair, and continues talking as though at confession.*)My mother used to send my father out to get water from the street pump. We were hopelessly poor. We lived in Zyrardow on Victory of the Revolution Street. Father would take the bucket and go straight to the bar on Glorious Future Street. He'd check his bucket in the cloakroom. There'd always be about thirty buckets hanging there on the hooks. At midnight they'd close the bar and that's when my mother would send me to get Father. I was fourteen then. One night when I was dragging Father home, he pretended not to know who I was. That was on Saint Marks . . . I mean, Karl Marx Street. There were no street lights and it was always so dark.

HE. You see what you've done to my wife? Who are you anyway? What did you come here for? (*The BUM looks through his pockets for something.*)

SHE. Five years ago a journalist from *Der Stern* asked me whether I'd like to be fourteen years old again. Those Germans can't get Faust out of their heads. But it put me into a cold sweat. I told him that would be the worst joke life could play on me. A person's got the strength to make such a climb only once in a lifetime. (*The BUM pulls something out of his pocket that looks like an ID card wrapped in several layers of paper napkins. He hands the bundle to him. HE starts to unwrap it with great care.*)

SHE. In my case, this remake of *Faust* doesn't work very well. The devil was furious because I left Poland. I refused to make a deal with him. So in revenge he screwed up my brain. Now here I am . . . fourteen again and back in Zyrardow. I've lost everything except my accent. (*HE finishes the unwrapping, revealing the content of the bundle. It is an empty plastic case, the dimensions of an ID card.*)

HE. There's nothing in it.

BUM. (*check's for himself and agrees with Jan*) That's right. (*He takes the plastic cover out of Jan's hand, carefully rewrapping it in the paper napkins, then puts it back in his pocket. Next he starts to crawl slowly under the bed.*) Your wife will calm down once you're in the park. (*to HER*) Hold out your hands. (*to HIM*) See?

SHE. See what? (*She looks at her hands which don't shake.*)

BUM. What do you mean, see what?

SHE. Are they shaking?

HE. I don't know. Maybe not. Maybe just a little.

BUM. (*ironically*) Is that what you call "just a little"? When I first moved to our park, my nerves were just like yours. Now take a look at my hands. (*The BUM stretches out both hands which shake terribly. Triumphantly:*) How about that?

HE. I don't know. How can I put it . . .

SHE. Your hands are shaking.

BUM. Are you kidding? (*He looks at JAN who nods in consent. Astounded:*) Do you really think so?

HE. Can't you see for yourself?

BUM. (*looking at his hands*) Well, maybe just a little bit. That's nothing. You should have seen my hands before. They'll straighten out once I get back to the park, you'll see. (*disappears under the bed*)

SHE. Oh, God. Maybe he knows that we'll end up in the park.

HE. How could he know that?

SHE. (*looking at her hands*) How did those secret policemen know we were going to leave Poland? Go see Zbyszek right away. Ask him to lend us money to pay the rent. (*HE fails to react.*) Did you hear? (*HE whistles.*) What's going on?

HE. He won't lend us any money.

SHE. He promised he would.

HE. You see, it seems Zbyszek didn't have a work permit.

SHE. What do you mean he didn't have a work permit?

HE. He was using a forged card. Strictly illegal. He and a Turkish worker.

SHE. Good God.

HE. Someone turned them in as illegal aliens. Immigration officers raided the Statue of Liberty and arrested Zbyszek and the Turk, in the torch. (*HE shakes his head negatively.*)

SHE. But if they send Zbyszek back to Poland, he'll be put in jail immediately.

HE. Maybe not immediately.

SHE. Janek . . .

HE. Yes?

SHE. Maybe it's punishment.

HE. What punishment?

SHE. That we can't sleep . . . Punishment for running away from Poland.

HE. Nonsense. They threw us out.

SHE. We could've resisted . . . Janek . . .

HE. What now?

SHE. Maybe we should pray.

HE. What?

SHE. But why not? Let's just try. It wouldn't hurt. I mean, the Pope is a Pole.

HE. But God isn't.

SHE. Let's pray.

HE. What an idea!

SHE. Do it for me. As a favor. (*They awkwardly try to find a place to kneel.*)

HE. OK. What language should we pray in? In Polish or in English?

SHE. It doesn't make any difference.

HE. I don't know how to pray in English.

SHE. Let's start with "Our Father who art in heaven . . ."

HE. What are we praying for?

SHE. For us to fall asleep.

HE. Maybe . . .

SHE. What?

HE. Let's start with something easier than that . . . if it works then we'll ask for more.

SHE. For a green card.

HE. Think so?

SHE. Sure! (*They both concentrate on praying.*)

HE. (*After a moment:*) I can't.

SHE. But why not?

HE. Oh Christ!

SHE. For God's sake don't be sacrilegious.

HE. I'm ashamed to pray for a green card. (*HE turns out the light.*)

SHE. No Janek. You can't give up. Listen, this is America. (*chasing a cockroach*) Ugh . . . (*SHE squashes it by pounding it with her shoe against the floor. From the floor below comes the sound of pounding on the ceiling with the broom.*)

HE. Oh, damn. A knocking from below.

SHE. So what. It means we haven't fallen to the very bottom yet. At least somebody is still below us.

HE. Strange it didn't occur to me until now. Of course,

in Milton and Baudelaire termites, sometimes other insects, rhythmically beat their heads against the floor to inform the hero of his imminent death. In Genet too . . . You appeared in Genet's plays, do you remember?

SHE. I don't think the cockroaches would warn us. And you know that it's the old hag downstairs who keeps knocking.

HE. In Goethe's *Faust* knocking precedes the coming of Mephistopheles from hell.

SHE. But she's from Lithuania. (*in desperation*) Why don't you write? Dear God, just think, a morbid brain like yours is being wasted. We could afford to buy a house if you only knew how to sell those obsessions of yours. If you can't write a full-length book, write something, one line at least, something to the point like "McDonald's—we do it all for you." It might be that our bed is standing over a vein of water which alters the magnetic field, and that in turn causes our insomnia. Let's change the position of the bed . . .

HE. We already did that only yesterday.

SHE. Let's do it again. The vein of water can change its course and follow every move we make . . . I bought you that book, *Money Is My Friend*, and you haven't even opened it yet.

HE. You didn't buy it, you found it in the trash. You expect me to learn how to make money by reading a book which someone else threw out in the garbage.

SHE. Maybe that person had already made his money and got rid of the book when he didn't need it any more.

HE. I wanted to tell you that at first when I arrived in America I was self-possessed, I tried hard, if only you'd behaved differently.

SHE. I did everything you asked me to. You said one

can't get anywhere in America without being in the phone book, so I took care of it. *I* took care of it. We're in the phone book, Krupinski, only no one calls us.

HE. Please do forgive me, but I'd like to remind you that it was due to me, and to all the time and effort that I put into it, that the Thompsons ever came to visit us. And you know that they're friends with . . .

SHE. (*interrupting him*) You're not going to start that over again, are you?

HE. I kept begging you to get a grip on yourself. And at least for that one evening to behave decently. I mean, you know they're very close to . . .

SHE. (*interrupting him*) You asked me to do something quite different.

HE. What'd I ask you to do?

SHE. To keep my mouth shut and not to say anything bad about socialism, Jaruzelski, Gorbachev and the Soviet Union.

HE. If you say bad things about it, they'll say you're a classic example of paranoia affecting emigres.

SHE. If I say good things about them, they'll ask me why I left Poland.

HE. I ask you not to say *anything* on the subject, only to make a good impression. That's all. The Thompsons are good people on whom a lot depends. They could change our entire life, they could help us find a publisher for my new book, they could introduce us to . . .

SHE. What new book? I think . . .

HE. You can think anything you want, but just don't say it.

SHE. The Secret Police in Poland said exactly the same thing.

HE. Just who do you think you are? The conscience of the nation?

(*An American couple crawl out from under the bed. They are both very elegantly dressed, in evening clothes. Mr. THOMPSON brings with him two folded blankets in a plastic bag. Mrs. THOMPSON, who is trying unsuccessfully to conceal her fear of the surroundings, carries a small, beautifully wrapped gift. As the THOMPSONS appear from under the bed, the conversation in the room is drawing to a close.*)

HE. And please, don't change.
SHE. Why?
HE. You look fine just as you are.
SHE. Why?
HE. You should look totally natural.
SHE. Why?
HE. To arouse their compassion. (*SHE disappears into the bathroom, slamming the door. HE puts on a jacket and glasses. HE, turning to the THOMPSONS*) I'm so glad you've come. We really appreciate it that you found the time to drop by and pay us a visit. Welcome, welcome.

MR. THOMPSON. (*picking the two folded blankets in a plastic bag off the floor*) No, no, it's up to us to welcome you to America. Welcome, welcome. You look wonderful. Last time I saw you, you had me somewhat worried. Right, dear?

MRS. THOMPSON. Oh, yes. (*Exchange of handshakes, during which Jan's hand leaves ink smudges on the THOMPSONS' hands. MR. THOMPSON pretends he doesn't notice anything while MRS. THOMPSON tries to wipe the ink off with a handkerchief.*)

HE. They took our fingerprints. For the green card. They of course suspect us of being spies.

MR. THOMPSON. Of course. I mean . . . I'm sorry to hear that. All these formalities are so awful.

HE. I don't know. It's not so bad. It's just difficult to get the ink off afterwards.

MRS. THOMPSON. (*with growing fear in her eyes, speaking unnaturally loudly as if to make her English understandable*) It's a very nice apartment.

HE. We're still furnishing it. We're going to put an armchair over there, and a rug here. And a chair somewhere.

MRS. THOMPSON. It's already very nice and cozy as it is. Besides, I read in the *Times* that the neighborhood is getting better and better.

HE. Oh, yes, yes, the neighborhood. My wife's in the bathroom. Excuse me, I'll go get something to drink. Make yourselves at home.

MRS. THOMPSON. Oh, that's very nice of you. I'd just like a cup of tea, please. (*Her eyes rest on the used teabags hanging on the rope to dry.*) Or just a glass of water.

HE. Of course, right away.

MR. THOMPSON. If you'd seen our first apartment, my dear boy. Am I right, dear? (*MRS. THOMPSON bursts out in nervous laughter.*)

MR. THOMPSON. I have the feeling you'll make it here. (*Jan is busy in the kitchen.*)

MRS. THOMPSON. Did you see those people in front of the building? I'm afraid they'll break into our car.

MR. THOMPSON. You can't judge people by appearances.

MRS. THOMPSON. I know, but I left my fur coat in the car. Good God, take a look at that bathtub.

MR. THOMPSON. Sshhh. You've got to be very careful of what you say, dear, or you'll hurt their feelings.

MRS. THOMPSON. Look, there's not a single painting.

MR. THOMPSON. But they're very brave. I'm sure they'll get a painting soon. And please, dear, don't say good things about socialism in their presence.

MRS. THOMPSON. (*astonished*) But socialism is a noble idea!

MR. THOMPSON. I know, dear, I know. But they've suffered a lot over there. And if they say something good about Reagan, don't be upset.

MRS. THOMPSON. What do you mean?

MR. THOMPSON. (*soothingly; looks around*) Yes, we'll invite them over some day soon. We'll introduce them to . . . It's our moral responsibility. They are interesting people. There's a sense of mystery about them. For example, he's written such a strange, dark novel.

MRS. THOMPSON. But you haven't even read it.

MR. THOMPSON. I'll read it during my vacation.

HE. (*to MR. THOMPSON*) I'm awfully sorry, I don't know what happened, I'd like to do something to help, but a bottle of vodka got misplaced somewhere. Oh, I've got some sleeping pills. I hid them from my wife somewhere. (*HE bustles around the bed, finds a bottle of sleeping pills and shakes it joyfully.*) Here they are. But you don't have any trouble sleeping, do you?

MRS. THOMPSON. I didn't know your wife suffers from insomnia.

HE. No, no, it's nothing serious. My wife and I always sleep at the same times.

MRS. THOMPSON. That's wonderful.

HE. (*in Polish*) Wyjdziesz wreszcie, czy nie. Oni zaraz sobie pojdą.

MR. THOMPSON. By the way, we brought you two blankets which might come in handy sometime. And . . . a small nothing, more symbolic than anything else. (*MRS. THOMPSON hands to Jan an ele-*

gantly wrapped replica of the Statue of Liberty. He unwraps it and examines it enraptured, then places it along several identical ones.)

MRS. THOMPSON. I've heard that your wife is an actress.

MR. THOMPSON. My wife knows a lot of people in the theatre. We'll try to help.

HE. That'd be wonderful. (*shouts*) Anka, hurry up, will you?

MRS. THOMPSON. What kind of roles does she appear in?

HE. Mainly the classical repertory. Women in Shakespeare.

MR. THOMPSON. Women in Shakespeare . . . Then we've definitely got to call Joe.

MRS. THOMPSON. Has your wife got an accent?

HE. (*proudly*) Of course. She doesn't have a work permit. But she's got an accent.

MRS. THOMPSON. Well, after all no one knows what Elizabethan English actually sounded like.

HE. That'd be wonderful. (*knocks at the bathroom door*)

MR. THOMPSON. Is your wife a member of Equity?

HE. I don't know about that.

MRS. THOMPSON. Of course in order to perform in New York you wife first has to become a member of Equity. But of course in order to become a member of Equity your wife must have performed in New York.

HE. (*confused*) Of course.

MRS. THOMPSON. There is a certain way of circumventing this regulation. I mean it could be done as a cultural exchange between our two governments. Let's say your wife would go back to Poland . . . let's say for one year, and the Polish government would arrange a

HUNTING COCKROACHES

performance for her in New York, at the same time inviting as a cultural exchange an outstanding American actress to perform in Warsaw. Simple!

HE. But we have emigrated from Poland.

MRS. THOMPSON. Yes. That can be an obstacle.

MR. THOMPSON. Tell me quite frankly, what do you think of us.

HE. What do I think of you?

MR. THOMPSON. You can be straight with me. (*pause. They look at each other.*) Do you like America?

HE. Oh, we think it's a great country and wonderful too.

MR. THOMPSON. Of course. But you must understand that not everything in America is as wonderful as it looks.

HE. No?

MR. THOMPSON. No. You see, all the emigres who come here are above all grateful, as you yourself noticed, for the boundless opportunities and for the sense of freedom and security that America offers them. That's only understandable.

HE. I should say so.

MR. THOMPSON. I'm connected with a publishing house which is interested in a slightly different view of America. A more complex view, a more probing view . . . a darker view, if you will . . .

HE. I will . . .

MR. THOMPSON. . . . a view which would show us what we Americans have lost . . . For I am of the opinion that you emigres have got something that we don't.

HE. We do?

MR. THOMPSON. Yes, you do.

HE. What's that?

MR. THOMPSON. A soul.

HE. A soul?

MR. THOMPSON. A soul. I've mentioned your name to the publisher. Are you interested?

HE. In writing a book about having a soul?

MR. THOMPSON. No, a book about not having a soul.

HE. I'm definitely interested. Do you think they'll give me an advance immediately?

MR. THOMPSON. (*somewhat irritated*) Submit a chapter or two first . . . I'm sure you'll write it in no time at all. I can imagine with all the new impressions you've been gathering, you must be a volcano of energy.

HE. (*clenching his fists energetically*) Oh, yes.

MR. THOMPSON. You looked around the streets. Haven't you noticed?

HE. Yes, there is something I haven't seen. But it's a lot of wonderful things . . .

MR. THOMPSON. (*correcting him*) The dark side.

HE. Yes, absolutely!

MR. THOMPSON. Look at the subway.

HE. I agree. The graffiti for example. It's hooliganism. In Poland they would never allow it.

MR. THOMPSON. I'm afraid that here I have to disagree. Graffiti is a popular form of a true folk art which expresses the soul.

HE. The soul?

MR. THOMPSON. In certain places we still have some left.

MRS. THOMPSON. (*screams*) Aaaa . . .

MR. THOMPSON. What happened?

HE. What happened?

MRS. THOMPSON. Nothing, absolutely nothing, everything's all right. I simply need a glass of water.

HE. I'll get it for you right away. (*runs over to the kitchen*)

MR. THOMPSON. What was it, dear?

MRS. THOMPSON. There's a rat under the bed.

MR. THOMPSON. What do you mean a rat?

MRS. THOMPSON. A rat. (*screams*) Look, there it is! (*points with her finger*)

HE. (*returning with a glass of water in his hand*) Did something happen?

MR. THOMPSON. No, nothing at all. Just a rat who ran under the bed.

HE. Oh, please, don't worry, that's not a rat, just a big mouse.

MR. THOMPSON. There, you see.

MRS. THOMPSON. (*again in an exaggeratedly loud voice*) It was a rat. It's got a very long, hairless tail.

HE. You can believe me, it's a big mouse. Mice frequently have long, hairless tails. I know what I'm talking about. I've already started a book . . .

MR. THOMPSON. Oh, that sounds wonderful.

HE. A book about a Polish writer who comes to New York and plans to kill a rich old woman who lives on Park Avenue. He argues that she has no right to go on living . . .

MRS. THOMPSON. (*appalled*) Why does he think that?

HE. (*animated*) He maintains he knows better than she does how to make use of her money. He's planning to kill her with an axe. (*HE demonstrates. MR. and MRS. THOMPSON exchange bewildered glances.*) Of course, my book owes a certain debt to Dostoyevsky. But unlike Dostoyevsky's hero, the hero in my book doesn't kill the old woman. In fact, she turns out to be a very charming old lady . . . She seduces him, he falls in love with her, and then . . . they go to this . . . this . . . Florida together . . . Because here in America the general situation and opportunities are quite different than in Russia. (*He stops a moment and notices disgust on the faces of his guests.*) I suppose it might be in bad taste, mightn't it? . . . That's why I stopped working on it.

(*The bathroom door is flung open. From inside out rolls the wheelchair with HER in it. She's wearing the costume of a nineteenth century Polish emigre. A scarf around her head. A huge shawl wrapping her body tightly; huge oversized boots, a missing front tooth. She's distinctly pregnant. A bottle of vodka in her hand. With a friendly smile she wheels the chair towards the THOMPSONS.*)

MR. THOMPSON. I'm so pleased to meet you. You look wonderful. (*He stretches out his hand. SHE tries to kiss it. Pulling his hand away:*) I'm so pleased to meet you. (*SHE squeezes MRS. THOMPSON's hand leaving ink smudges on it.*)

MR. THOMPSON. Courageous people . . . I didn't realize that your wife . . . (*Meanwhile Anka, making friendly gestures and patting the bottle of Vodka fondly, invites them to the table, mumbling something in Polish.*)

HE. It's nothing serious.

MR. THOMPSON. There are still many roles: *The Glass Menagerie* . . . *Sunrise at Campobello* . . . *Richard III*. (*He crawls under the bed.*)

MRS. THOMPSON. (*crawling under the bed*) I think you're going too far. Yesterday it was American Indians and now it's Polish emigres. It's really too much.

SHE. I'm sorry but I can't stand compassion. And I really don't like suffering. And I hate that Dostoevsky of yours and all his heroes who commit frightful deeds and then with their hands folded in prayer voluntarily go off to Siberia, accept suffering and become saints. I never

HUNTING COCKROACHES

wronged anyone, I don't want to suffer and I reject feelings of compassion. (*HE takes Vodka into kitchen. SHE speaks to audience.*) Oh, God, how very amusing I used to be when I first came to this country. I was the center of attention at parties. I'd tell jokes. Everyone would say how bright I was. I'd quote the Talmud. But now all I want to do is to cut their throats. That's why I'd like to go into business. (*HE returns.*) Anyway you could have written that chapter or two and have showed them to him. I still don't understand why you don't.

HE. What could I write about America when for over a year I haven't ventured beyond 4th Street. (*SHE turns light on.*) How long has it been since we stopped being able to sleep?

SHE. Shortly after we came to America, at first I couldn't sleep for something like a month, then I could, and then I couldn't again. Oh, my front tooth's hurting again . . . Since when did we stop sleeping together?

HE. 385 days ago.

SHE. Are you sure you really wouldn't like to have a tiny little creature with grey-blue eyes? (*HE remains silent.*) I mean, a little kid like that would greet you every time you came home.

HE. We don't go out anymore. (*HE gets back in bed. SHE follows him.*)

SHE. But we could start going out again at night. We'd reach an agreement with the cockroaches since they sleep during the day and hunt at night. That way we wouldn't bother one another anymore. What do you think?

HE. I wonder how cockroaches propagate?

SHE. Come cuddle closer.

HE. Do they make love in the normal way?

SHE. I'm sure cockroaches go see horror movies about people, and then after the movies, they kiss and hop into bed.

HE. I read somewhere that cockroaches are all female . . . I didn't want to tell you.

SHE. Now you're starting all over again.

HE. . . . and that they propagate by cellular division . . . they don't need a male.

SHE. You're talking pure nonsense. (*HE doesn't move.*) By cellular division . . . (*SHE turns out the light.*)

(*The CENSOR appears in the middle of the bed.*)

CENSOR. I'm from the Central Bureau of Censorship. I mean the Central Office of Human Relations. (*He smiles.*) I would like to invite you back to Poland. We will of course publish all your work.

HE. But you took my apartment away from me.

CENSOR. Your apartment has been renovated. Our interior decorator allowed himself to refurnish it Victorian style, which I remember, from the last play of yours we banned, you like very much. Haven't you heard about the changes in our country? Haven't you been reading the New York Times? Your English must be good enough by now.

HE. Wait a minute. You're not my censor. I know my own censor, don't I?

CENSOR. You mean Tadek? Poor guy, he has been transferred. He wasn't open minded enough . . . too inflexible. We are retraining him. Here are two plane tickets for you and your wife, first class of course! And food and gasoline coupons for the first two years.

HE. I appreciate it very much.

CENSOR. You're very welcome.

HE. Yes, but for how long? I'm very sorry. I don't know how to put it, but I wasn't born yesterday. You know, I've seen it all before.

CENSOR. You've got no conscience.

HE. Yes, I do.

CENSOR. No, you've got no conscience.

HE. Maybe I've got no conscience but I've got a memory. (*HE gives the tickets back.*)

CENSOR. Maybe you've got a memory but you'll never write anything in the States.

HE. And what makes you so sure?

CENSOR. I've gone through all your notes. They don't lead anywhere—except maybe to the Lower East Side. And let me tell you in confidence, two thousand dissident immigrants, all of them prominent, have just been put on a jumbo jet in Moscow and are leaving for New York. They are all carrying the very same stuff you brought. I've gone through all their notes, too. And I can tell you that they are all very talented. Whatever you say, Gogol, Dostoevski, Tolstoy—that's some heritage! Maybe you can help them find a publisher. I wish all of them the best of luck. We believe that a short stay on the Lower East Side is a priceless experience for our free thinkers. (*HE gives the tickets back again.*) No? Are you sure? (*CENSOR looks around, takes off his jacket and is wearing a Hawaiian shirt underneath. He takes off his bureaucrat's glasses and replaces them with sunglasses.*) Listen—if you want to stay, let's go into business together. I know the American market. I'll be your agent. We don't want to crack-up in this nasty room, do we? Call my secretary—we'll do lunch. (*CENSOR exits. HE turns on the light.*)

HE. Anka, Anka, wake up!

SHE. What happened?

HE. I think I had a nightmare.

SHE. That's great! That means you fell asleep. Now everything will be alright for us. Now you can start to write. (*HE lies down in the bed, gives her a dirty look and pulls the blanket over his head. SHE looks at HIM for a moment, then she opens the closet and pulls out a big suitcase. SHE opens it and starts to throw her personal belongings into it.*)

HE. (*From under the covers.*) What are you doing?

SHE. We're packing.

HE. (*Sitting up in the bed.*) Again?

SHE. Just keep quiet, don't say anything.

HE. But, Anka.

SHE. Be quiet.

HE. We can't go back.

SHE. Yes, we can.

HE. They won't let us back in.

SHE. They will.

HE. And even if they do let us in, they won't ever let us out again.

SHE. So, they won't.

HE. We'll lose all our contacts. Just when everything is starting to work out for us . . . (*Without interrupting HER packing, SHE gives HIM a dirty look. Embarrassed, HE avoids HER gaze.*) . . . —They'll say we're coming back, because we didn't make it here, because we're failures.

SHE. We are failures.

HE. They'll make fun of us.

SHE. So they'll make fun of us.

HE. They took our apartment.

SHE. We'll stay with friends.

HE. And what about the plane tickets?

SHE. The tickets can be arranged. For Polish zlotys. On credit. Remember Janek, now we're dealing with

Poland. Everything can be fixed. People still remember us. I'll go on stage again. You'll write again.

HE. They won't publish it.

SHE. But you'll have something to write about. (*SHE throws the replicas of the Statues of Liberty into a suitcase and tries to close it.*) You see how lucky we are. All our belongings fit into one suitcase. (*SHE sits on the suitcase, trying to close it that way.*)

HE. No, that's no possible . . . It doesn't make any sense. I just don't know . . . Anyhow, (*Sits on the suitcase beside HER*) if we're going, we've got to call . . . (*Just at that moment the suitcase closes with the loud snap. They embrace.*)

SHE. Did you know that now you can call Poland direct just by dialing the country code? And the rates are cheaper this early in the morning.

HE. How much?

SHE. $1.40 a minute.

HE. You call that cheap? 4.20 for three minutes?

SHE. No. Each additional minute is 40 cents. So it'd be only 2.20 for 3 minutes. Anyway, Janek, we are going back. God, I'm so happy. Just think how happy they'll be. Let's call Jurek. Where's my address book?

HE. But Jurek is in Australia.

SHE. Not Jurek.

HE. Yes, Jurek. He emigrated to Australia.

SHE. Are you sure? How's he doing in Australia?

HE. He's doing very well.

SHE. Acting?

HE. He works as a gas station attendant.

SHE. That means he got a work permit. When did he leave Poland?

HE. A year ago. It's much easier to get a work permit in Australia.

SHE. What about calling Andrzej?

HE. Andrzej is in Paris.

SHE. Then how about Basia?

HE. Basia's in prison.

SHE. Maybe Bolek?

HE. Bolek hanged himself.

SHE. That's right. I knew that.

HE. Maybe Rysiek.

SHE. What are you talking about? He became a collaborator, nobody even shakes his hand now. (*SHE crosses out his name in her address book.*) Let's call Irena!

HE. That's not such a good idea.

SHE. Why not?

HE. Zbyszek called her the other day and she hung up on him. Her telephone is bugged. And besides, she just got out of the clink. She's scared and sick.

SHE. I can understand that she didn't want to talk to Zbyszek. But I was her best friend . . .

HE. You know, they say I'm working for the CIA . . .

SHE. I forgot. We should write to CIA and ask them to forward our check. (*SHE picks up the telephone. Their euphoria about the trip to Poland wanes.*)

HE. Anyway, better not put her on the spot. She'll feel awful if she hangs up on you, and if she doesn't, she may get into trouble. (*SHE dials 12 numbers.*) Who are you calling? (*SHE doesn't answer.*) Tell me.

SHE. It's exactly 12:25 PM in Poland now. I just called.

HE. 12:25?

SHE. 12:26 now. (*Hangs up the phone. They lie for several moments in silence. HE turns off the light. The room remains in darkness. After a moment SHE appears in a spotlight on the forestage and addresses the audience.*) This is a secret but tomorrow I have this audition, well, maybe not tomorrow, I'm not quite ready yet. It's to be a stand-up comedienne . . . you know . . . like on TV . . . I have this really funny piece. Okay . . . A blind man and a man with only one eye were crossing the river in a boat. The blind man did the rowing and the man with only one eye steered. In the middle of the river, the blind man accidentally swung his oar out of the water and hit the man with only one eye in his good eye. "This is the end," said the man who used to have only one eye. The blind man thought they'd reached the other shore and stepped out of the boat. (*SHE waits, smiling, for the audience's reaction, then bows several times, ending with a Shakespearean flourish.*)

BLACKOUT

THE END

PRONUNCIATION OF POLISH NAMES AND WORDS

Unless otherwise indicated, Polish names and words are accented on the next to last syllable.

Anka:Ań-ka
Janek: Yá-neck
Krupinski: Kru-pín-ski
Andrzej: Ańd-zhay (zh sound as in azure)
Spytaj o pieniądze: Spée-tie o pyen-yaẃnd-say
Lech Wałęsa: Lech (ch as in Scottish loch) Va-wen-sa
Tomek: Tó-meck
Krzysiek: Kshí-sheck
Grazyna: Gra-zhée-na (zh as in azure)
Zosia: Zó-sha
Włodek: Vwó-deck
Zbyszek: Zbí-sheck
Gdansk: Gdánsk
Rysio: Rí-show
Czesio: Chés-show
Miodowa: Myoo-dó-va
Marciniak: Mar-cheén-yak
Stalinowka: Sta-lin-off-ka
Stalinowo: Sta-lin-ó-vo
Małgosia: Mau-gó-shah
Zyrardow: Zhir-aŕ-douf (Zh as in azure)
Wyjdziesz wreszcie, czy nie. Oni zaraz sobie pojdą.: Veéd-yesh
vrésh-cheh, chi nye. Ó-ni zá-raz só-bye poí-dawn.
Tadek: Tá-deck
Jurek: Yoú-reck
Basia: Bá-shah
Bolek: Bó-leck
Rysiek: Rí-sheck
Irena: Ear-eń-a
Ah, ah, kot-key dva, shar-ray, boo-ray, o-bid-va . . .

PROP PRESET

D.R. Table (*upside down*)
3 Liberties
Sewing kit w/needle threaded

Antennae
Basket w/clothing (babushka on top)
and Statue of Liberty

S.R. Table (angled position)
2 Pads
2 Pencils
2 Books
2 Dishes
1 Mug
8 File cards
2 Forks
2 Spoons
2 Knives
2 Napkins

Chair

Wicker Chair

Lamp w/
Jan's Jacket

Wardrobe w/ (top catch done)
Janek's coat
Wallet w/ 3 ID cards in pocket
Anka's dress, hangers

Wheelchair
Footrest down

Bed w/
3 Pillows
Blankets—1
Bedspread—1
Sheets—2
Pills (in mattress pocket)
Shoe—mid R. edge
Shoe—nr. head, L.
Hanky—under S.R. pillow

Night table w/
Diary
Pencil
Handkerchief } in
Stuff } drawer
TV
Antennae in

Shelves
Award
Liberties
3 Books
Pictures

Boxes w/
Amber jewelry
Faust
Assorted clothing, books, etc.
Phone book

HUNTING COCKROACHES

Desk
NY Times reviews — 2
Vill. Voice reviews — 2
Lamp
Phone
Scissors   } in
Clothes brush } drawer

Desk chair

Map of U.S.

Footlocker w/
Newspapers
(2 single sheets on top)

Refrigerator
4 Glasses   } on
Ashtray w/aspirin } top
Clothespin
Dressing inside

Cabinets
Teapot w/H$_2$O
Milk carton
2 Mugs
1 Glass w/H$_2$O

On upstage [off] rail:
2 Pr. stockings
Dishtowel
Mug w/teabag

Charcoal under U.L.C. chair rail
Bath door closed
Shower curtain ½ open
Plug out of deck

Off right
I Folder w/   (IMMIGRATION OFFICER)
   Immigration papers
   Stamp pad
   Pens
   Notebook & pen   (RYSIO)
   Gun & holster   (CZESIO)
II Bum's cart w/   (BUM)
   Plastic ID case (wrapped in paper towels)
   Pint of booze
   Blankets in plastic case   (MR. THOMPSON)
   Charcoal   (MRS. THOMPSON)
   2 Airline tickets ⎫
   Business card   ⎬   (CENSOR)
   Coupons   ⎭
   Censor's box by trolley

For ACT II preset:
Hanky w/orange oil
Map of Europe
L. pencils
Decaf teabag
Roach spray
Jan's eyeglasses
Address book

D.R. Table (upside down)
3 Liberties
Sewing kit w/ needle threaded

HUNTING COCKROACHES

Antenna
Basket w/ babushka on top (triangle)

S.R. Table (angle)
2 Yellow pads & pencil
2 Books
8 Note cards
2 Plates, 2 sets flatware on 2 napkins

Chair, wicker chair

Bath door closed—sweatshirt & scarf on hook
Tub curtain ½
Schmutz U.L.C. under chair rail
Pole lamp
Jan's jkt

Wardrobe
Jan's coat—wallet w/ 3 ID's in pocket
3 Hangers—dress
Top catch

Wheelchair
Facing D.S., footrest down

Off R.
I   Immigration papers (replace)   } Folder
    Stamp pad (charcoal)

II   To go on
    Hanky & orange oil
    Map o' Europe
    2 Pencils
    Bum's cart w/ pint bottle (H$_2$O)

68 HUNTING COCKROACHES

Decaf Teabag
Roach spray
Jan's glasses & case
Address book (replace Tues.)
ID. case in paper towel
Blankets in plastic case
Cig case (7 Carlton regs), lighter
Liberty—pink box
Plane tickets, fuel coupons, business card
Censor's box by trolley

Off U.L. (bath)
Dish towel
3 Pr. hose
Mug w/ teabag

Bed
3 Pillows (She—2, He—1)
2 Sheets (wash 1)
Striped blanket
Bedspread
Pill bottle in pkt
Shoes—1 DS., 1 US.
Check skirt
Hanky—under her pillow

Night table
Comp book
Pencil
Handkerchief } drawer
Stuff
Save toothwax

TV
Antenna in

Shelves
Award
Liberties
3 Books

S.L. Boxes
Amber jewelry
Faust
Phone book
Folded clothes

Desk (chair face VS.)
2 Ea. reviews (Times, Voice)
Lamp (down, plugged in)
Phone (D.L. corner, plugged in)
Scissors }
Lint brush }   drawer
3 Legal pads, pencil
Map of U.S.

Footlocker
Newspapers
2 Single sheets on top

Refrigerator
4 Glasses
Ashtray w/ aspirin
Green clothespin

Off U.C.
Teapot (H_2O), 2 mugs
1 Glass (H_2O)
Milk carton

INTERMISSION

Set
Roach spray — L. of bed
3 Pencils, map (Europe), mug w/t — desk
Handkerchief (orange oil) — night table drawer
Address book — box L.

Reset
TV — L.
Wicker chair
Phone
Lamp up
Phone book CL.R.
Pill bottle on night table
Table R. straight
Bed — on spike, tidy
Wardrobe — jacket in, bottom catch, rig tieline
Push back shower curtain
Desk chair face L.
Green clothspin — fridge
Shoe — shelf of night table
ID cards — coat pocket
Kitchen towel to fridge

Strike
Milk carton
Babushka
Glasses

Off
Bum's cart — under bed
Jan's glasses — kitchen
2 Glasses (H_2O)
Vodka bottle (H_2O)

COSTUME PLOT

SHE (Anka)

Matching full length robe & nightgown in pale floral print cotton
Heavy wool athletic socks (white)
Wedding band

Props

Small black & pink floral wool scarf (for head)
Large black & pink floral wool shawl with fringes
Large pillow for "pregnancy"

HE — Janek

Grey sweat pants
Waffle weave long underwear shirt (beige)
Dark blue plaid flannel shirt
Black cotton athletic socks
Gold wire rim glasses
Wedding band

Add in Thompson's scene:
   Brown tweed 3-button sports jacket

ACT ONE

IMMIGRATION OFFICER

Black wool/polyester trousers
Black leather belt w/gold buckle
White cotton/polyester long sleeve shirt w/pens & shirt guard in pocket
Large gold watch on expansion bracelet
Black tie w/gold tie clip
Black socks
Black loafers

CZESIO

Grey pin stripe, 3 button polyester suit
"Lenin" pin on lapel
Wide maroon tie
Black leather belt
Grey & orange striped long sleeve shirt
Black arm sling
Cheap watch w/large face
Black socks
Heavy black shoes

RYSIO

Brown polyester sport trousers
Brown belt
Black shiny polyester shirt w/rush & white "chain" pattern
Brown leather short jacket
Brown leather cap
Short black zippered boots
Brown socks

ACT TWO

BUM

2 Pair of distressed jeans — bell-bottoms over straight legs
Beige T-shirt w/vegetable design
Grey zippered sweat shirt — distressed
Jean vest
Plaid shirt worn as belt through jeans
Ace bandage (dirty) around outside of knee
Black torn/distressed raincoat w/green stripe lining
Distressed blue boat shoes

MRS. THOMPSON

3 Piece "Chanel" style evening suit in flat black sequins trimmed w/gold bugle beads
Skirt
Jacket
Sleeveless top
Black & gold high heeled pumps
Black beaded purse w/gold trim
Sheer black stockings
Rhinestone jewelry:
  Drop earrings
  2 Large stone rings

MR. THOMPSON

Black tropical weight wool tuxedo & full accessories
Pleated shirt w/spread collar
Black enamel studs & cuff links
Black silk cummerbund & bow tie
Patent leather tie shoes
Black knee socks
White breast handkerchief

CENSOR

Polish army uniform w/ribbons & silver stars — "Polish Eagles" on lapels
Black socks
Black uniform shoes
White silk scarf at neck

Under dressed
  Hawaiian shirt in yellow & red
Round wire framed glasses

Floor Plan

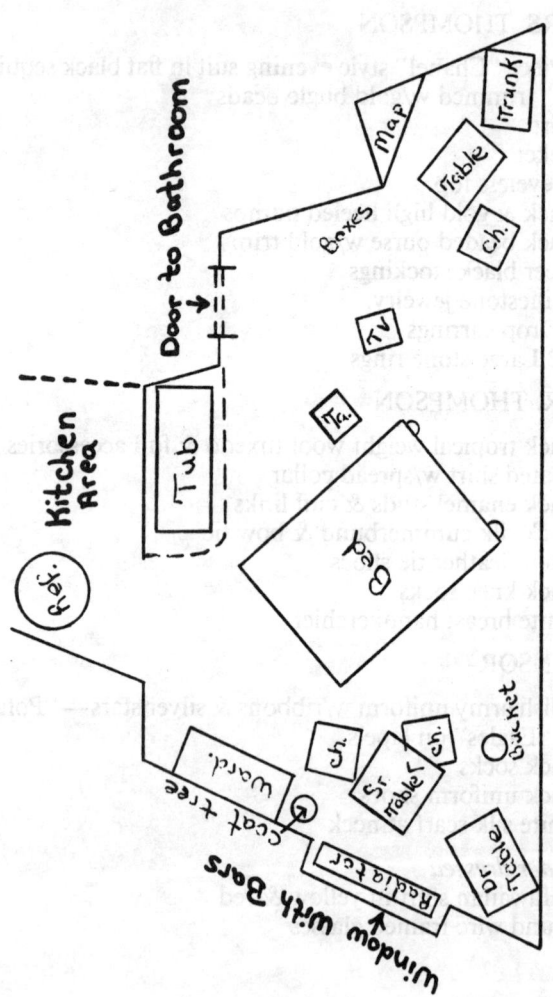

Other Publications for Your Interest

THE CURATE SHAKESPEARE AS YOU LIKE IT
(LITTLE THEATRE—COMEDY)
By DON NIGRO

4 men, 3 women—Bare stage

This extremely unusual and original piece is subtitled: "The record of one company's attempt to perform the play by William Shakespeare". When the very prolific Mr. Nigro was asked by a professional theatre company to adapt *As You Like It* so that it could be performed by a company of seven he, of course, came up with a completely original play about a rag-tag group of players comprised of only seven actors led by a dotty old curate who nonetheless must present Shakespeare's play; and the dramatic interest, as well as the comedy, is in their hilarious attempts to impersonate all of Shakespeare's multitude of characters. The play has had numerous productions nationwide, all of which have come about through word of mouth. We are very pleased to make this "underground comic classic" widely available to theatre groups who like their comedy wide open and theatrical. (#5742)

SEASCAPE WITH SHARKS AND DANCER
(LITTLE THEATRE—DRAMA)
By DON NIGRO

1 man, 1 woman—Interior

This is a fine new play by an author of great talent and promise. We are very glad to be introducing Mr. Nigro's work to a wide audience with *Seascape With Sharks and Dancer*, which comes directly from a sold-out, critically acclaimed production at the world-famous Oregon Shakespeare Festival. The play is set in a beach bungalow. The young man who lives there has pulled a lost young woman from the ocean. Soon, she finds herself trapped in his life and torn between her need to come to rest somewhere and her certainty that all human relationships turn eventually into nightmares. The struggle between his tolerant and gently ironic approach to life and her strategy of suspicion and attack becomes a kind of war about love and creation which neither can afford to lose. In other words, this is quite an offbeat, wonderful love story. We would like to point out that the play also contains a wealth of excellent ***monologue*** and ***scene material.*** (#21060)

Other Publications for Your Interest

CAT'S PAW
(LITTLE THEATRE—DRAMA)
By WILLIAM MASTROSIMONE
2 men, 2 women—Interior

This is a gripping drama about terrorism; but it does not come at the subject in a way you'd expect. When we think of "the terrorist", we generally think of a wild-eyed religious or political fanatic. What if, posits the acclaimed author of *The Woolgatherer*, *Extremities*, *Shivaree* and *Nanawatai*, a terrorist came along who was brilliant, who was articulate and who was *right*? Victor is the head of a terrorist group which is responsible for a bomb attack against the White House in which 27 people have been killed. He has arranged to have a television news reporter led to his lair, there to tell the world why he has done what he has done. Victor's obsession is the destruction of the world's water supply, and with it the final destruction of the human race, by pollution. When the reporter asks him if he feels any guilt about the death of the 27 innocent people, he replies that hundreds of innocent people are dying every hour because of what mankind is doing to its water supply—and do the people responsible feel guilt for this? This cat-and-mouse game between the young woman reporter and Victor gets more and more tense, leading to a shocking and violent conclusion. A standing-room-only hit at Seattle Repertory Theatre and later at San Diego's Old Globe. "An agonizingly suspenseful thriller."—San Diego Tribune. "A grabber."—Seattle Times. "Timely, thought-provoking and definitely worth seeing."—San Diego Reader. "Entertaining, informative, thoughtful and scary."—The Weekly (Seattle). (#5056)

SHIVAREE
(LITTLE THEATRE—COMIC DRAMA)
By WILLIAM MASTROSIMONE
2 men, 3 women—Combination interior

We are delighted to publish this lesser-known but wonderful play by the acclaimed author of *Extremities* and *The Woolgatherer*. The story concerns a young hemophiliac youth named Chandler who has been kept, of necessity, by his cab driver mother in a very sheltered sort of existence. Chandler is desperate for contact with the world. He is also highly intelligent; but is supremely naive about the ways of the world. He pays a neighbor to bring him a girl; but he can't go through with his plans to have sex with her. He just doesn't know what to do about his craving for love—until he meets Shivaree. She is another neighbor who supports herself by being an itinerant belly-dancer. She is a True Original, and before too long the delightful Shivaree and the innocent Chandler are in love, much to the consternation of Chandler's mother, who forbids Chandler to ever see Shivaree again, throwing Shivaree out of Chandler's room. Chandler, undaunted, climbs out the fire escape—his first venture outside his hermetic world—going after his love. Fans of Mr. Mastrosimone's other plays will recognize the true-ness of the characterizations and the poignancy and humor of typical Mastrosimone dialogue in this wonderful play. (#21689)

Other Publications for Your Interest

NOISES OFF
(LITTLE THEATRE—FARCE)
By MICHAEL FRAYN
5 men, 4 women—2 Interiors

This wonderful Broadway smash hit is "a farce about farce, taking the clichés of the genre and shaking them inventively through a series of kaleidoscopic patterns. Never missing a trick, it has as its first act a pastiche of traditional farce; as its second, a contemporary variant on the formula; as its third, an elaborate undermining of it. The play opens with a touring company dress-rehearsing 'Nothing On', a conventional farce. Mixing mockery and homage, Frayn heaps into this play-within-a-play a hilarious melee of stock characters and situations. Caricatures—cheery char, outraged wife and squeaky blonde—stampede in and out of doors. Voices rise and trousers fall . . . a farce that makes you think as well as laugh."—London Times Literary Supplement. ". . . as side-splitting a farce as I have seen. Ever? *Ever.*"—John Simon, NY Magazine. "The term 'hilarious' must have been coined in the expectation that something on the order of this farce-within-a-farce would eventually come along to justify it."—N.Y. Daily News. "Pure fun."—N.Y. Post. "A joyous and loving reminder that the theatre really does go on, even when the show falls apart."—N.Y. Times. (#16052)

THE REAL THING
(ADVANCED GROUPS—COMEDY)
By TOM STOPPARD
4 men, 3 women—Various settings

The effervescent Mr. Stoppard has never been more intellectually—and *emotionally*—engaging than in this "backstage" comedy about a famous playwright named Henry Boot whose second wife, played on Broadway to great acclaim by Glenn Close (who won the Tony Award), is trying to merge "worthy causes" (generally a euphemism for left-wing politics) with her art as an actress. She has met a "political prisoner" named Brodie who has been jailed for radical thuggery, and who has written an inept play about how property is theft, about how the State stifles the Rights of The Individual, etc., etc. Henry's wife wants him to make the play work theatrically, which he does after much soul-searching. Eventually, though, he is able to convince his wife that Brodie is emphatically *not* a victim of political repression. He is, in fact, a *thug*. Famed British actor Jeremy Irons triumphed in the Broadway production (Tony Award), which was directed to perfection by none other than Mike Nichols (Tony Award). "So densely and entertainingly packed with wit, ideas and feelings that one visit just won't do . . . Tom Stoppard's most moving play and the most bracing play anyone has written about love and marriage in years."—N.Y. Times. "Shimmering, dazzling theatre, a play of uncommon wit and intelligence which not only thoroughly delights but challenges and illuminates our lives."—WCBS-TV. 1984 Tony Award-Best Play. (#941)

Other Publications for Your Interest

A WEEKEND NEAR MADISON
(LITTLE THEATRE—COMIC DRAMA)
By KATHLEEN TOLAN

2 men, 3 women—Interior

This recent hit from the famed Actors Theatre of Louisville, a terrific ensemble play about male-female relationships in the 80's, was praised by *Newsweek* as "warm, vital, glowing . . . full of wise ironies and unsentimental hopes". The story concerns a weekend reunion of old college friends now in their early thirties. The occasion is the visit of Vanessa, the queen bee of the group, who is now the leader of a lesbian/feminist rock band. Vanessa arrives at the home of an old friend who is now a psychiatrist hand in hand with her naif-like lover, who also plays in the band. Also on hand are the psychiatrist's wife, a novelist suffering from writer's block; and his brother, who was once Vanessa's lover and who still loves her. In the course of the weekend, Vanessa reveals that she and her lover desperately want to have a child—and she tries to persuade her former male lover to father it, not understanding that he might have some feelings about the whole thing. *Time Magazine* heard "the unmistakable cry of an infant hit . . . Playwright Tolan's work radiates promise and achievement." (#25051)

PASTORALE
(LITTLE THEATRE—COMEDY)
By DEBORAH EISENBERG

3 men, 4 women—Interior
(plus 1 or 2 bit parts and 3 optional extras)

"Deborah Eisenberg is one of the freshest and funniest voices in some seasons."—Newsweek. Somewhere out in the country Melanie has rented a house and in the living room she, her friend Rachel who came for a weekend but forgets to leave, and their school friend Steve (all in their mid-20s) spend nearly a year meandering through a mental landscape including such concerns as phobias, friendship, work, sex, slovenliness and epistemology. Other people happen by: Steve's young girlfriend Celia, the virtuous and annoying Edie, a man who Melanie has picked up in a bar, and a couple who appear during an intense conversation and observe the sofa is on fire. The lives of the three friends inevitably proceed and eventually draw them, the better prepared perhaps by their months on the sofa, in separate directions. "The most original, funniest new comic voice to be heard in New York theater since Beth Henley's 'Crimes of the Heart.'"—N.Y. Times. "A very funny, stylish comedy."—The New Yorker. "Wacky charm and wayward wit."—New York Magazine. "Delightful."—N.Y. Post. "Uproarious . . . the play is a world unto itself, and it spins."—N.Y. Sunday Times. (#18016)

Other Publications for Your Interest

KNOCK KNOCK
(LITTLE THEATRE—FARCE)
By JULES FEIFFER

3 men, 1 woman—Composite interior

Take a pair of old Jewish bachelor recluses, throw in Joan of Arc who also in another life was Cinderella—add another character who appears in various guises and you have the entire cast but not the story of this wild farce. Cohn, an atheistic ex-musician is the housekeeper "half" of this "odd couple." Abe, an agnostic ex-stockbroker is the practical "half." They have lived together for twenty years—are bored to tears with one another and constantly squabble. Cohn, exasperated, wishes for intelligent company and on the scene enters one Wiseman who appears in many roles and is part Mephistopheles, part Groucho Marx. Then Joan of Arc appears before the couple telling them her mission is to recruit two of every species for a spaceship trip to heaven. After that all antic hell breaks loose and continues to the mad ending. "... a wild spree of jokes ... helium-light laughter."—Clive Barnes, N.Y. Times. "... a kooky, laugh-saturated miracle play in the absurdist tradition."—Time. "... grand fun, possessed by a bright madness ..."—N.Y. Post. "... a knockout of original humor."—NBC. "... intelligent and very funny play."—WABC-TV.

LITTLE MURDERS
(ALL GROUPS—COMEDY)
By JULES FEIFFER

6 men, 2 women—Interior

"Jules Feiffer, a satirical sharpshooter with a deadly aim, stares balefully at the meaningless violence in American life, and opens fire on it in 'Little Murders.' ... Can be devastatingly lethal in some of its coldly savage comic assaults." (N.Y. Post). The play is really a collection of what Walter Kerr called set pieces, showing us a modern metropolitan family of matriarchal mother, milquetoast father, normal cuddly sister, and brother who is trying to adapt himself to homosexuality. Sister's fiance is a fellow who knows how to roll with the punches; he figures that if you daydream while being mugged, it won't hurt so much. They have a hard time finding a preacher who will marry them without pronouncing the name of God. But they succeed, to their sorrow. For immediately afterward sister is killed by a sniper's bullet. A detective who has a stack of unsolved crimes suspects that there is "a subtle pattern" forming here. "'Little Murders' is fantastically funny. You will laugh a lot."—N.Y. Times. "You have made me laugh, you have made me collapse. I want to go back."—N.Y. Post. "One of the finest comedies this season.—NBC-TV.

Other Publications for Your Interest

TALKING WITH...
(LITTLE THEATRE)
By JANE MARTIN

11 women—Bare stage

Here, at last, is the collection of eleven extraordinary monologues for eleven actresses which had them on their feet cheering at the famed Actors Theatre of Louisville—audiences, critics and, yes, even jaded theatre professionals. The mysteriously pseudonymous Jane Martin is truly a "find", a new writer with a wonderfully idiosyncratic style, whose characters alternately amuse, move and frighten us always, however, speaking to us from the depths of their souls. The characters include a baton twirler who has found God through twirling; a fundamentalist snake handler, an ex-rodeo rider crowded out of the life she has cherished by men in 3-piece suits who want her to dress up "like Minnie damn Mouse in a tutu"; an actress willing to go to any length to get a job; and an old woman who claims she once saw a man with "cerebral walrus" walk into a McDonald's and be healed by a Big Mac. "Eleven female monologues, of which half a dozen verge on brilliance."—London Guardian. "Whoever (Jane Martin) is, she's a writer with an original imagination."—Village Voice. "With Jane Martin, the monologue has taken on a new poetic form, intensive in its method and revelatory in its impact."—Philadelphia Inquirer. "A dramatist with an original voice . . . (these are) tales about enthusiasms that become obsessions, eccentric confessionals that levitate with religious symbolism and gladsome humor."—N.Y. Times. *Talking With . . .* is the 1982 winner of the American Theatre Critics Association Award for Best Regional Play. (#22009)

HAROLD AND MAUDE
(ADVANCED GROUPS—COMEDY)
By COLIN HIGGINS

9 men, 8 women—Various settings

Yes: *the Harold and Maude!* This is a stage adaptation of the wonderful movie about the suicidal 19 year-old boy who finally learns how to truly *live* when he meets up with that delightfully whacky octogenarian, Maude. Harold is the proverbial Poor Little Rich Kid. His alienation has caused him to attempt suicide several times, though these attempts are more cries for attention than actual attempts. His peculiar attachment to Maude, whom he meets at a funeral (a mutual passion), is what saves him—and what captivates us. This new stage version, a hit in France directed by the internationally-renowned Jean-Louis Barrault, will certainly delight both afficionados of the film and new-comers to the story. "Offbeat upbeat comedy."—Christian Science Monitor. (#10032)

NEW OFF BROADWAY HITS
from
SAMUEL FRENCH, INC.

THE ALTO PART—BETWEEN DAYLIGHT AND BOONVILLE—BETWEEN NOW AND THEN—BIG MAGGIE—BLOOD MOON—BLUE WINDOW—CINDERS—CLARA'S PLAY—CRIMINAL MINDS—EDMOND—EXTREMITIES—FEN—THE FLIGHT OF THE EARLS—THE FREAK—GENIUSES—GREATER TUNA—HACKERS—HOMESTEADERS—THE HOUSE OF RAMON IGLESIA—HUSBANDRY—KNUCKLEBONES—LAST DAYS AT THE DIXIE GIRL CAFE—LIVING QUARTERS—LUNCH GIRLS—NURSE JANE GOES TO HAWAII—PASTORALE—QUARTERMAINE'S TERMS—ROMANCE LANGUAGE—SHIVAREE—SPLIT SECOND—TOP GIRLS—A WEEKEND NEAR MADISON—WE WON'T PAY! WE WON'T PAY!—THE WORKROOM—ZELDA

For details, consult our *Basic Catalogue of Plays*.

THE SAMUEL FRENCH THEATER BOOKSHOP

SAMUEL FRENCH, INC. (New York)
45 West 25th Street
New York, NY 10010
(212) 206-8990 (FAX 212-206-1429)
(open 9:00-5:00, Mon.-Fri.)

SAMUEL FRENCH, INC. (California)
7623 Sunset Blvd.　　　11963 Ventura Blvd.
Hollywood, CA 90046　　Studio City, CA 91604
(213) 876-0570　　　　(818) 762-0535
FAX 213-876-6822
(call for hours)

SAMUEL FRENCH (Canada) LTD.
80 Richmond Street East
Toronto, Ontario M5C 1P1
CANADA
(416) 363-3536
(open 9:00-5:00, Mon.-Fri.)

SAMUEL FRENCH LTD. (England)
52 Fitzroy Street
London W1P 6JR
England
011-441-387-9373　FAX 011-441-387-2161
(open 9:30-5:30, Mon.-Fri.)

Specializing in plays and books on the theater

ISBN 0 573 69052 9　　　　　　　　#10166